# TRACING YOUR IRISH ANCESTORS THROUGH LAND RECORDS

## A Guide for Family Historians

## CHRIS PATON

Pen & Sword

**FAMILY HISTORY**

First published in Great Britain in 2021 by
**PEN AND SWORD FAMILY HISTORY**
An imprint of
Pen & Sword Books Ltd
Yorkshire – Philadelphia

ISBN 978 1 52678 021 8

Printed and bound in the UK by TJ Books Ltd,
Padstow, Cornwall.

Pen & Sword Books Limited incorporates the imprints of Atlas,
Archaeology, Aviation, Discovery, Family History, Fiction, History,
Maritime, Military, Military Classics, Politics, Select, Transport,
True Crime, Air World, Frontline Publishing, Leo Cooper, Remember
When, Seaforth Publishing, The Praetorian Press, Wharncliffe
Local History, Wharncliffe Transport, Wharncliffe True Crime
and White Owl.

For a complete list of Pen & Sword titles please contact

# CONTENTS

# INTRODUCTION

When carrying out ancestral research in Ireland, we traditionally start in the most recent years with the civil registration records generated by the state, north and south, which document births, marriages and deaths, and then try to travel further back in time with the use of parish records of varying denominations. Many of the problems that we might encounter along the way are caused by a range of issues, including the very existence of such records at certain periods in the past, and the details, or lack of, contained within those that have survived. Other resources may help to plug the gaps where the vital records fail, but perhaps none can do so more than land and property records, in their many varied forms.

Whilst our ancestors have come and gone through history, the landscape of Ireland itself has towered over everything as a constant. The very soil around us, the environment that nurtures us, is as much a silent witness to much that has gone on before our time as the DNA that leads us onwards from within. At times, the story of the island has intruded into our ancestral stories directly, motivating our ancestors' passions and struggles for justice, whilst at other moments in the past it has stood by passively, silently observing, and providing a background context to other stories at play before it.

I was born in the County Antrim town of Larne, and was raised for much of my childhood in the nearby borough of Carrickfergus. Today I live just across the water from 'Carrick' on the Ayrshire coast in Scotland, but to root the idea of my ancestral origins as an Ulsterman into my two boys, I once told them, when they were very young, that I owned the mighty Norman edifice that is Carrickfergus Castle, and that I was its king! The truthful reality is that for a couple of years as a small child I had simply lived in a small house just along the road from the castle.

Our home in the town's Robinson's Row was inherited by my father in 1979 from my grandmother Jean Paton (née Currie) after she had passed away, and was the same property within which he had previously been raised as a wee boy himself many years earlier. For two years, we endured freezing trips to its outdoor toilet, based in a shed across the backyard, and lived in a house with no bathroom or shower, with just a single tap in the house producing water that had to be boiled on the gas cooker to wash with. Many people had regular baths; we had regular basins! To my father, who had just left the Royal Navy after fifteen years of service, it was now a relic from another era which was not suitable to raise his own children within. By the early 1980s, we had moved on to one of the new housing estates at the north end of the town, with a property boasting central heating, large outdoor gardens, and most impressively, an indoor loo and bathroom.

Following the passing of my father in early 2021, in the midst of the coronavirus pandemic (sadly a factor in his death), I took possession of many items that he had acquired across his life. Amongst these were the will left by my grandmother, and additional correspondence from her in the lead up to its being drafted in 1975. One of her concerns was the interesting question on what basis she actually owned her house at Robinson's Row, and whether she was still liable for any ground rent attached to it. A response from her solicitor addressed the point as follows:

> I am pleased to confirm that having inspected your title deeds under which you hold the premises at 2 Robinson's Row it only reserves a rent of 5p a year if demanded and the premises could therefore be regarded as being freehold although legally that is not strictly the case. For all practical purposes, however, there is no ground rent to pay.

These documents were a testimony to the preparations for her own demise, the passing on of the property that had been her sole remaining companion for many years once her children had all grown up and fled the coop. Photographs held by my father showed the obvious pride and joy that he had as a young teenage boy whilst there, and of my grandmother as the owner of her wee home. Whilst I was never the king of Carrickfergus Castle, no-one could argue that Jean Paton was most certainly the queen of Robinson's Row.

In many records, such as street directories or censuses, a family may pop up briefly at an address and disappear again soon after, whilst in other ancestral branches, there may be properties that have remained within a family for decades, and even centuries, which may be mentioned repeatedly in such documents. But how often do we pay any actual

*The author's grandmother Jean Paton peering out from her Carrickfergus home at Robinson's Row.*

*The author's father, Colin Paton, as a teenager at the front door of his home at Robinson's Row.*

attention to the places described, in our searches to discover who might be related to who? If you ignore the context of where our ancestors lived, you will be assuredly missing out on a key part of the family narrative.

This book is a much expanded revision of a short guide previously written for Australian-based firm Unlock the Past. With it I hope you will be able to learn about, and find, the records that can help to determine the history of land and property within Ireland, as a means to both aid your genealogical pursuits and to provide an ancestral canvas against which your family findings can be displayed. It will discuss where to seek such records in Ireland itself, as well as the increasing range of collections that can be found online.

It is my hope that in so reading this book you will begin to realise that when it comes to Irish research, whether in the north or the south, the glass is most definitely half-full and not half-empty. Even if the records described in this work cannot help directly once plundered, it might still help you to ask the right questions.

Finally, a huge thanks from this uncrowned king of Carrickfergus Castle to my wife Claire, and sons Calum and Jamie, for their ongoing support, and to all at Pen and Sword who have helped to pull the volume before you together, including Gaynor Haliday for her work as editor. This book is dedicated to the memory of my father Colin Paton (1945–2021).

As ever, I hope this work will help to reveal the greatest Irish story that you will ever know – your very own.

Chris Paton

# TIMELINE

The following timeline provides some key dates and events from the last five centuries in Ireland, which I hope can act as a ready reckoner for genealogical and land history research.

*Pre-Union*

| 1529 | Tudor Conquest commences |
| 1556 | Laois and Offaly Plantations |
| 1583 | The Plantations of Munster |
| 1606 | Hamilton-Montgomery Settlements in Antrim and Down |
| 1609 | The Plantations of Ulster |
| 1652 | Act of Settlement |
| 1654–6 | Civil Survey of Ireland |
| 1656 | Down Survey of Ireland |
| 1659 | Sir William Petty's census (Pender's Census) |
| 1702 | Creation of the State Paper Office to hold records of the Lords Lieutenant of Ireland (the Crown's representatives in Ireland) |
| 1704 | Act to Prevent the Further Growth of Popery |
| 1708 | Registry of Deeds established in Dublin |
| 1715 | County Palatine of Tipperary Act |
| 1778 | Catholic Relief Act |
| 1782 | Catholic Relief Act |
| 1793 | Catholic Relief Act |
| 1798 | United Irishmen rebellion |

*The United Kingdom*

| 1801 | Ireland joins Britain to form the United Kingdom of Great Britain & Ireland |
| 1813–15 | First national census of Ireland attempt fails |
| 1821 | First successful Irish decennial census – few records survive |
| 1823 | Composition for Tithes Act; tithes now to be paid with money |

| 1826 | Valuation of Land (Ireland) Act – enabled Townland Valuation from 1830 |
| 1829 | Roman Catholic emancipation |
| 1831 | Decennial census – few records survive |
| 1831–6 | Tithe War |
| 1832 | Representation of the People Act |
| 1833 | Church Temporalities (Ireland) Act 1833; parish cess abolished |
| 1838 | Tithe Rentcharge Act; tithe rate reduced and incorporated into rent payments |
| 1838 | Poor Relief (Ireland) Act – creation of new state-based poor law system |
| 1841 | Decennial census – few records survive |
| 1843 | Commission on Occupation of Land (Ireland) (Devon Commission) |
| 1845–52 | Irish Famine (*An Gorta Mór*) |
| 1845 | Civil registration of non-Roman Catholic marriages commences |
| 1846 | Rateable Property (Ireland) Act – enabled Tenement Valuation (Griffith's Valuation) |
| 1848 | Encumbered Estates Act |
| 1849 | Encumbered Estates Act; Encumbered Estate Court established |
| 1849 | Renewable Leaseholds Conversion Act |
| 1851 | Decennial census – few records survive |
| 1852 | Landed Estates Court established |
| 1852 | Valuation (Ireland) Act – enabled publication of Griffith's Valuation |
| 1857 | Probates and Letters of Administration Act (Ireland) |
| 1861 | Decennial census – no records survive |
| 1864 | Civil registration of all births, marriages and deaths commences |
| 1867 | Creation of the Public Record Office of Ireland |
| 1870 | Landlord and Tenant (Ireland) Act |
| 1871 | Disestablishment of the Church of Ireland (Irish Church Act 1869) |
| 1871 | Decennial census – no records survive |
| 1877 | Foundation of the National Library of Ireland |
| 1877 | Land Judges Court established |
| 1879–82 | Land War |
| 1879 | Irish National Land League founded |
| 1881 | Decennial census – no records survive |
| 1881 | Land Law (Ireland) Act; Irish Land Commission established |
| 1885 | Purchase of Land (Ireland) Act (Ashbourne's Act) |
| 1887 | Land Law (Ireland) Act (Balfour's Act) |

| 1891 | Decennial census – no records survive |
| 1891 | Purchase of Land (Ireland) Act |
| 1898 | Local Government (Ireland) Act – major boundary & local governance reform |
| 1901 | Decennial census – records have survived |
| 1903 | Land Purchase (Ireland) Act (Wyndham's Act); addressed absentee landlordism |
| 1909 | Land Purchase (Ireland) Act (Birrel Land Act) |
| 1911 | Decennial census – records have survived |
| 1912 | Signing of the Ulster Covenant |
| 1914–18 | First World War |
| 1916 | The Easter Rising |
| 1919–21 | The War of Independence |
| 1921 | First *Dáil Éireann* formed |
| 1920 | Government of Ireland Act |
| 1921 | No decennial census carried out |
| 1921 | Partition of Ireland and creation of Northern Ireland |

*Post Partition*

| 1922 | Irish Civil War – destruction of the Public Record Office of Ireland |
| 1922 | The Free State of Ireland exits from the UK |
| 1923 | Land Law (Commission) Act 1923 (Free State); reconstituted Land Commission |
| 1923 | Creation of the Public Record Office of Northern Ireland |
| 1925 | Northern Ireland Land Act; established Land Purchase Commission (Northern Ireland) |
| 1926 | First post-Partition censuses in Northern Ireland and the Free State (northern records have not survived) |
| 1929 | Northern Ireland Land Act |
| 1933 | Land Act (Free State) |
| 1935 | Northern Ireland Land Purchase (Winding Up) Act |
| 1937 | Constitution of Ireland; renames the Free State as 'Ireland' (Éire) |
| 1937 | Northern Ireland census – records have survived |
| 1937 | Land Purchase Commission (Northern Ireland) dissolved |
| 1939–45 | Second World War (The Emergency) |
| 1939 | National Identity Register (Northern Ireland) |
| 1949 | Ireland formally becomes a republic (Republic of Ireland Act 1948) |
| 1965 | Land Act (Republic of Ireland) |

| | |
|---|---|
| 1970 | Land Registration Act (Northern Ireland) |
| 1988 | Formation of the National Archives of Ireland (from a merger of the Public Record Office of Ireland and the State Paper Office) |
| 1999 | Irish Land Commission in the Republic dissolved |
| 2009 | Land and Conveyancing Law Reform Act (Republic of Ireland) |
| 2011 | New PRONI building opens at Titanic Quarter, Belfast |

## Chapter 1

# THE LIE OF THE LAND

There are many types of record that can assist us in identifying which of our ancestors were related to whom, and to determine a more fleshed out family history for them. With such documents we can determine to whom we are related, where they once lived, what they once did for a living, and how they contributed to our ancestral heritage, all of which has led to our very existence. The purpose of this first chapter, however, is to provide some background information on some of the most commonly used sources for Irish land, property and house history research.

Many genealogical resources, but by no means all, are easily accessible online. To help to find those that are, I would recommend my book *Tracing Your Irish Family History on the Internet (Second Edition)* from Pen and Sword, in which I cover the basic record types, and also provide guides to useful websites on a province by province, and county by county, basis. For tips on how to make your research findings work better for you, and to generate further leads from them, I would also recommend my book *Sharing Your Family History Online*.

If until now you have primarily only been using online sites to carry out research, there are a wealth of archives, libraries, museums, and other repositories which await you with treasures aplenty. Whilst they may not deliver instantaneous results with the click of a button, they are certainly a lot of fun to explore, and in many cases will be the only place where you can access the relevant materials to assist with your enquiries.

One major point to really hammer home up front is that despite the island's Partition in 1921, which was cemented from 1922 onwards, Ireland's archives do not hold materials for their own local or national 'patches' only. For example, you will find many records concerning Northern Ireland at the National Archives of Ireland in Dublin, and many resources concerning people and places from the Republic of Ireland within the Public Record Office of Northern Ireland in Belfast (and not just for the three counties of Ulster on the other side of the border). In many cases, former landowners owned estates across Ireland, and following Partition they were not necessarily going to divide their records up before depositing them with an archive for safekeeping.

From a researcher's point of view, it is certainly wise to acknowledge that Partition happened, but in terms of looking for resources, consider the whole island as your plaything – there may well be treasures awaiting you where you might least expect them!

### National Archives of Ireland / An Chartlann Náisiúnta
Bishop Street, Dublin 8, Ireland
**www.nationalarchives.ie**

The modern National Archives of Ireland (NAI) facility was formed in 1998 following a merger of the Public Record Office and the State Paper Office.

Ireland's original Public Record Office was established in 1867 at the Four Courts in Dublin, but was unfortunately blown up during the opening stages of the Civil War in 1922. A great deal of material was lost, including many Church of Ireland records, court records, censuses and probate registers. The Reports of the Deputy Keeper of the Public Records in Ireland from 1867 to 1922, available to read at **https://beyond2022.ie/ ?page_id=1049#treasury** (scroll down to 'PROI Reports, 1867-1922' at the bottom right of the page), document what was previously held at the facility before its destruction. A major Decade of Centenaries project seeking to reclaim some of these resources, through conservation work of surviving damaged material and the sourcing of surrogates from partner institutions, is Beyond 2022 (**https://beyond2022.ie**).

The good news is that not everything was lost in 1922. Many copies of records have since been found that replace those that were destroyed, and of course, the archive has continued to acquire materials for the Free State and then the Republic, from Partition to the present day. In addition, a variety of indexes and finding aids to some of the materials which were lost have also survived. The NAI website hosts detailed research guides that can help to understand the records it currently holds, which can be found within various areas on its website, including the 'Historical records', 'Genealogy' and 'Legal records' sections.

In order to determine specific items which might be held at the facility, the archive's online catalogue is a useful workhorse. Amongst the most useful resources that have been catalogued are probate records and compensation claims from those who lost property during the revolutionary period. The catalogue allows you to carry out a 'Simple Search', using basic keywords only, or through an 'Advanced Search' function, which allows you to add a year range and other fields. On the results pages, results can be re-ordered alphabetically, by year or by reference code in ascending or descending order. The online catalogue holds 2 million documented items, although the facility notes that additional records have yet to be included which only exist in hard copy-based catalogues located on site.

The institution on Bishop Street is open from Mondays to Fridays, from 10 a.m. to 5 p.m. Some materials are held in off-site storage, and can be pre-ordered prior to a visit; off-site materials can be ordered in person when at the archive, but in such a circumstance they cannot be consulted until the following day. Free Wi-Fi is available, laptops can be used in the reading room, and materials can be photographed by researchers for personal use. A Reader's Ticket is required for research, with details on how to obtain one noted on the website.

The National Archives also has a separate genealogy records platform at **www.genealogy.nationalarchives.ie**, on which, at the time of writing, it hosts the following free-to-access collections:

- Census of Ireland, 1901 and 1911, and pre-1901 survivals
- Census Search Forms, 1841–51
- Tithe Applotment Books, 1823–37
- Soldiers' Wills, 1914–1918
- Calendars of Wills and Administrations, 1858–1922
- Prerogative and diocesan copies of some wills and indexes to others, 1596–1858
- Diocesan and Prerogative Marriage Licence Bonds Indexes, 1623–1866
- Catholic qualification & convert rolls, 1700–1845
- Valuation Office house, field, tenure and quarto books 1824–1856
- Shipping agreements and crew lists, 1863–1921
- Will Registers 1858–1900

Many of these collections can also be searched through partner sites such as FamilySearch, Findmypast, Ancestry and MyHeritage (p.14), sometimes offering a greater advantage than the archive's own platform, as will be noted later in this book.

The NAI also hosts many specialist projects online that might assist. These include the Chief Secretary's Office Registered Papers at www.csorp.nationalarchives.ie/index.html, which contains the registered papers of the Office of Chief Secretary of Ireland from 1818 to 1852, and the Colonial Office (Irish Branch) 1916 Easter Rising Compensation Files at http://centenaries.nationalarchives.ie/centenaries/plic, dating from 1917 to 1925, which lists claims for damages to property sustained during the revolutionary period, as administered by the Property Losses (Ireland) Committee.

On-site terminals at Bishop Street offer access to all of these databases.

**Public Record Office of Northern Ireland**
2 Titanic Boulevard, Belfast, BT3 9HQ
**www.nidirect.gov.uk/proni**

In 1923, a year after the destruction of Ireland's national archive, the Public Record Office of Northern Ireland (PRONI) was established in Belfast to serve as the main archival repository for the newly created state of Northern Ireland. Under the eyes of its first deputy keeper, D. A. Chart, a former employee of the PRO in Dublin, efforts were made to collect substitutes for much of the material lost concerning the north, including records sourced from solicitors, businesses, politicians, and even the aristocracy. As well as bringing in national government and court records for Northern Ireland, PRONI also collects local government records.

PRONI's website is a one-stop shop for everything that it offers by way of services to the public, hosting guides to records, an online catalogue, and digitised records. As with the NAI, the archive offers a series of useful topic guides on its records, the majority of which will be found within the section of the home page entitled 'Your research'. A particularly useful collection of topics for land and property research will be found under the 'Information' leaflets link.

PRONI's online eCatalogue is considerably more complete at the time of writing than its southern counterpart, but it is worth knowing that there are two different versions of this. It is possible to plan a great deal of research from home prior to attending, but on a first visit to the institution you will need an archivist to demonstrate the on-site version of the catalogue for you. Some digitised materials can be viewed at the institution using the catalogue, many of which are only accessible on site, and documents can be ordered up for consultation in the main documents' reading room.

The archive's online platform also hosts many free-to-access databases, including the following:

- Freeholders' records
- Londonderry Corporation records
- Name Search
- PRONI Historical Maps viewer
- PRONI Web Archive
- Street directories
- Ulster Covenant
- Valuation Revision Books
- Will calendars
- Absent Voters Lists

At the time of writing, only PRONI's 'Will calendars' database could also be accessed through a third-party site, via Ancestry's 'Web: Northern Ireland, Will Calendar Index, 1858–1965' collection.

Located in Belfast's Titanic Quarter, just a short walk from the city centre, PRONI is open from Mondays to Wednesdays and Fridays from 9 a.m. to 4.45 p.m. and on Thursdays from 10 a.m. to 8.45 p.m. As with the NAI, the building offers free Wi-Fi and plenty of sockets to plug in laptops, and also permits photography of holdings for personal use only. Researchers will again require a Reader's Ticket, details of which are outlined on the PRONI website.

The building also has an excellent on-site café.

*The Public Record Office of Northern Ireland in Belfast.*

**The National Archives (UK)**
Kew, Richmond, Surrey, TW9 4DU
**https://nationalarchives.gov.uk**

With the Republic of Ireland having been a constituent member of the United Kingdom from 1801 to 1922, and with Northern Ireland still a current member, The National Archives (TNA) of the UK at Kew, near London, may also be of some assistance. The archive's detailed 'Discovery' catalogue is accessible at **https://discovery.nationalarchives. gov.uk**.

Amongst TNA's many holdings is the archive's 'State Papers Ireland 1509–1782: Government Papers on Irish Affairs' collection, which has many useful letters written between the English (and then British) Crown and the Irish government in Dublin. A comprehensive guide to the collection, describing how it has been arranged, is listed at **www. nationalarchives.gov.uk/help-with-your-research/research-guides/ state-papers-ireland-1509-1782**. Some of the earlier sixteenth-century material has also been published by the Irish Manuscripts Commission (p.11). This TNA guide further includes information on other resources held on Ireland in British archives, including the Bodleian Library at the University of Oxford, Lambeth Palace Library, and the UK's Parliamentary Archives at Westminster.

Whilst many collections concerning Ireland at TNA are 'British' in scope and description, there are some gems specific to Ireland. For example, the Irish Sailors and Soldiers Land Trust was established after the First World War to build homes for ex-servicemen in Ireland, with over 4,000 properties built in the Free State from 1924 to 1932. After this point, no further properties were built in the south following a legal ruling of the Irish Supreme Court which prevented the Trust charging rent from ex-servicemen. By the 1980s, most properties created by the Trust in the Republic had been sold off. Additional properties were also built in Northern Ireland as late as 1952, and the Trust's work continued until its eventual abolition in 1987. The records at TNA, which include account ledgers and a property register, are catalogued by the archive under AP 1-8.

A useful article providing a general overview on holdings of Irish interest is 'Irish Records at the National Archives, Kew' by Audrey Collins, published in the *Irish Family and Local History Handbook 2* (Robert Blåtchford Publishing, 2013).

**National Library of Ireland** / Leabharlann Náisiúnta na hÉireann
Kildare Street, Dublin 2, Ireland
**www.nli.ie**

The National Library of Ireland (NLI) was originally founded in 1877 in Dublin as a body to host the collections of the Royal Dublin Society. Today it is a fully autonomous cultural institution, and cites its mission as being 'to collect, preserve, promote and make accessible the documentary and intellectual record of the life of Ireland and to contribute to the provision of access to the larger universe of recorded knowledge'.

The NLI is open from Mondays to Fridays from 10 a.m. to 4 p.m. at Kildare Street. The home page of the NLI's website offers a great deal of advice to help plan a visit, with various downloadable guides to help identify which holdings are available at the facility, many of which can be particularly informative for parish- and land-based resources. To consult materials in the various reading rooms you will need to have a Reader's Ticket.

The facility offers several useful finding aids and resources through the 'Catalogues & Databases' section of its website. Its main catalogue permits searches into journals, magazines, government publications, manuscripts that have been catalogued from 1990, and various visual print, drawing and photograph collections, including some 34,000 digitised glass plate negatives.

The NLI's Sources database at **http://sources.nli.ie** contains over 180,000 earlier pre-1990 catalogued records for Irish manuscripts, details of many other manuscript holdings documented as held in other institutions in Ireland and worldwide, and articles from various pre-1970 Irish periodicals. A database to help locate many newspaper resources, on site and across Ireland, is also accessible at **www.nli.ie/en/catalogues-and-databases-printed-newspapers.aspx**.

Amongst the library's most useful resources for land research are materials held by its Department of Manuscripts, which includes landed estate records collections and maps, for which there is a dedicated guide at **www.nli.ie/en/irish-landed-estates-rentals-and-maps.aspx**.

## Local archives, libraries and museums
The Republic of Ireland has various county archives and libraries which can further assist, but do bear in mind that local government websites are rarely comfortable within their own skins, and have a very frustrating habit of re-arranging the online furniture with alarming regularity, so you may need to update relevant bookmarks from time to time.

Contact details are too many to list here, but they are detailed in the county by county guide in my book *Tracing Your Irish Family History on the Internet (Second Edition)*. The Clare County Library has an exceptional site at **www.clarelibrary.ie/eolas/coclare/genealogy/genealog.htm**, for example, with a variety of online resources including censuses, tithes records, lists of freeholders, court records (including details of evictions), directories, and much more. The Archives and Records Association (Cumann Cartlann agus Taifead) platform at **www.araireland.ie** has an exceptional Archives Directory located under the Resources tab on the main menu, listing many archives and institutions across the island of Ireland.

Across Ireland, there are also many museums with special collections that may contain useful resources, many of which are also now finding their way online. In my home town in Co. Antrim, for example, Carrickfergus Museum has digitised a nineteenth-century transcription of the Old Town Records 1600–1800 and placed them online at **www.midandeastantrim.gov.uk/things-to-do/museums-arts/carrickfergus-museum-and-civic-centre/collections-and-research/carrickfergus-old-town-records-1600-1800**. These contain evidence of leases, expired

*The Irish Archives Resource can help to locate collections within repositories across Ireland.*

leases and grants of fee farm (p.103) throughout this period, as well as other historic documents, such as transcriptions of Crown charters, the earliest being one granted by Elizabeth I on 20 March 1569 to the town, under its former historic name of Knockfergus.

To find collections within the island's various city- and county-based archives, libraries and museums you can visit the site of the relevant repository itself or utilise the Irish Archives Resource website at **www.iar. ie**. Launched in early 2011, this provides a consolidated search platform for resources held by the Irish Capuchin Provincial Archives, Cork City and County Archives, Dublin City Archives, the Guinness Archive, the Irish Film Archive, the Irish Jesuit Archives, Limerick City Archives, NUI Galway JHL, the Public Record Office of Northern Ireland, the Royal College of Physicians of Ireland and UCC Boole Library Archives, as well as many county-based archives and other repositories. Direct links to the participating archives are located at **www.iar.ie/Links.html**.

A similar platform, which concentrates on library and university-based holdings, is the Research and Special Collections Available Locally (RASCAL) site at **www.rascal.ac.uk**. Initially designed for Northern Ireland, it was created as a means to provide information on research and special collections held by Queen's University Belfast, The University of Ulster, Library and Information Services Council (Northern Ireland), the Public Record Office of Northern Ireland, the Linen Hall Library and Belfast Public Libraries. It has since been extended to cover the whole of Ireland, and now details holdings of the Royal Irish Academy, University College Cork, Trinity College Dublin, Dublin City Public Libraries, and other institutions.

A full list of participating institutions can be found at **www.rascal. ac.uk/?func=aboutUs**, via the 'Institutions' tab on the left of the page. The 'Links' page also provides access to many of the partners' websites directly.

### Valuation Office / Oifig Luachála
Block 2, Irish Life Centre, Abbey Street Lower, Dublin 1, Ireland
**www.valoff.ie**

The Valuation Office in Dublin has an Archives and Genealogy service which provides information on all rateable properties in Ireland from the 1850s to the 1990s, including the Cancelled Land Books (p.60) which show changes of occupancy and ownership in the aftermath of Griffith's Valuation (p.91).

At the time of writing, records from the counties of Carlow, Cavan, Clare, Cork (City and County), Donegal, Dublin (City and County), Galway, Kerry, Kildare, Kilkenny, Limerick (City and County), Mayo, Meath, Monaghan, Offaly, Roscommon, Sligo, Tipperary and Wexford have been digitised, which can be viewed on a visit to the Public Office. An online enquiry service is also available.

The records of the Valuation Office are some of the most important for nineteenth-century Irish research in the Republic of Ireland, and will be discussed further in Chapter 5. The equivalent records for Northern Ireland are held at PRONI, which will be equally discussed.

### Property Registration Authority / An tÚdarás Clárúcháin Maoine
Chancery St, Dublin 7, Ireland
[Offices also at Golf Links Road, Roscommon, and Cork Road, Waterford]
**www.prai.ie**

The Property Registration Authority (PRA) handles enquiries on three major fronts: concerning the Land Registry (**www.prai.ie/land-registry-services**), the Registry of Deeds (**www.prai.ie/registry-of-deeds-services/#records**), and Ground Rents (**www.prai.ie/category/services/grservices**), including the ground rents purchase scheme (p.103). The agency holds records for the whole of Ireland prior to Partition, and for the Republic of Ireland after.

You can visit the PRA offices in Dublin, Roscommon and Waterford to identify plots for which you are seeking information through the Land Registry, although you can also carry out searches online (p.138).

For the Registry of Deeds, you can visit the agency's offices at Henrietta Street, Dublin, to carry out searches of the original records for the required fee. Many historic records can also be viewed online through digital microfilms created by FamilySearch (p.14), although the quality of these varies across microfilms.

As with Ireland's valuation records, the Registry of Deeds and the Land Registry are important resources for land and property research, and will be discussed in some depth in Chapter 6.

### Land and Property Services
Lanyon Plaza, 7 Lanyon Place, Town Parks, Belfast, Northern Ireland, BT1 3LP
[Other customer centres are based in Ballymena, Craigavon, Londonderry and Omagh]
**www.nidirect.gov.uk/articles/searching-the-land-registry**

The agency tasked with handling the Land Registry in Northern Ireland is Land and Property Services (LPS), which operates five customer service centres providing access to entries recorded in the Land Registry following Partition.

The centres can also be used to search for Northern Irish properties registered within the Registry of Deeds from 1923 to 1989 in paper format, and from 1990 onwards in digital format; earlier enquiries will need to be carried out at PRONI, or at the Registry of Deeds in Dublin.

To carry out searches you will need to obtain a permit from LPS, with details for this and the relevant search fees outlined on the website.

**Irish Manuscripts Commission**
45 Merrion Square, Dublin 2
**www.irishmanuscripts.ie**

The Irish Manuscripts Commission has been tasked since 1928 with disseminating information about the history and cultural heritage of Ireland. It has produced over 190 publications since it was founded, including its *Analecta Hibernica* series documenting shorter manuscripts, which is catalogued on the website.

Many of the Commission's most important publications have been reproduced in a free-to-access digital format on its website, including many volumes of the seventeenth-century *Books of Survey and Distribution* (p.83).

**Irish Architectural Archive / Cartlann Ailtireachta na hÉireann**
45 Merrion Square, Dublin 2
**https://iarc.ie**

The Irish Architectural Archive, also based at 45 Merrion Square, was established in 1976, and contains the largest architectural collection in Ireland, including books, pamphlets, photographs, documents and drawings from practices and repositories across the whole island. Details on how to register to use the Reading Room are available on its website.

The archive's website also hosts its extensive catalogue, as well as a user-friendly database: the Dictionary of Irish Architects. This is accessible at **www.dia.ie**, and contains biographical and bibliographical information on architects, builders and craftsmen working in Ireland from 1720 to 1940.

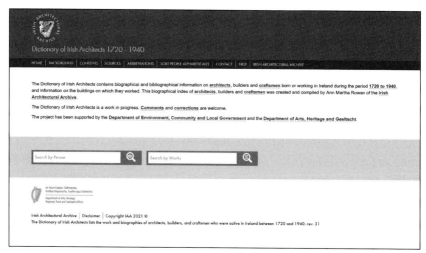

*The Dictionary of Irish Architects database from the Irish Architectural Archive.*

## Other heritage services

The National Inventory of Architectural Heritage was created in 1999 by the Irish government's Department of Housing, Local Government and Heritage, to identify, record, and evaluate the post-1700 architectural heritage of Ireland. The project's website at **www.buildingsofireland.ie** permits searches into two key ongoing surveys carried out by the Irish government – the 'Building Survey' and the 'Garden Survey' – which provide information on historic properties, accompanied by resources such as aerial photographs and maps, as well as its County Surveys.

The Northern Ireland Sites and Monuments database, which offers information on over 16,000 archaeological sites and historic monuments, is available at **https://apps.communities-ni.gov.uk/NISMR-PUBLIC/Default.aspx**

Northern Ireland's Heritage at Risk register (also known as the 'Buildings at Risk register') was established in 1993, and can be accessed at **https://apps.communities-ni.gov.uk/Barni/**.

For architectural drawings of Church of Ireland properties, the Representative Church Body Library – Architectural Drawings website at **https://archdrawing.ireland.anglican.org** can help.

## Place names

For the derivations of place names in Ireland, and for their pronunciation in both English and Irish, visit The Placenames Database of Ireland at **www.logainm.ie**. A useful glossary of commonly used place-name terms derived from the Irish language and distribution maps can be found at **www.logainm.ie/en/gls**.

A separate but similar endeavour for the north, The Northern Ireland Place-Name Project, has information on some 30,000 locations at **www.placenamesni.org**.

## Gateway websites

There are many so-called 'gateway sites' that can help to locate further useful online collections. Some of these specifically host records whilst others link to other platforms, meaning that occasionally dead links may appear. If such a link appears, it is worth searching for the named collection on a search engine such as Google to see if it might be available in another format elsewhere. It is also possible in some cases to visit 'dead' websites if the pages have been 'cached' on internet libraries such as the Internet Archive's 'Wayback Machine' at **https://archive.org/web/web.php**.

Dublin-based genealogist John Grenham's Irish Ancestors site (**www.johngrenham.com**) offers many excellent resources and tools which he previously created for the now defunct *Irish Times* site of the same name, some of which are free. His useful 'Placenames' tab allows you to locate the parish of a particular place of interest and to view it on a map. The 'Browse' area is the real workhorse of the site, however, which allows for the identification of record collections which may exist for a particular area, including shelf marks for library holdings and archive-held records, detailed lists of civil and Roman Catholic parish maps, and more. The 'Sitemap' page (**www.johngrenham.com/sitemap.php**) can readily take you to the area of interest without going through the menu-based tabs, whilst John's dedicated genealogy blog at **www.johngrenham.com/blog** is also well worth bookmarking.

Claire Santry's Irish Genealogy Toolkit at **www.irish-genealogy-toolkit.com** provides a handy introduction to some of the key record resources available for research in Ireland, north and south, as well as lists of useful contacts and downloadable free resources, such as charts and forms. Claire's blog, Irish Genealogy News (**www.irishgenealogynews.com**), is also well worth following.

Jane Lyons' From Ireland at **www.from-ireland.net** offers a range of free resources, the result of a research effort first started in 1996. Many record sets are transcribed, whilst the site also contains thousands of photographs and inscriptions taken in graveyards across the island. The various collections are accessible by following the grey links on the 'Explore' bar in the middle of the screen.

Several other sites provide county-based lists of transcribed records. These include:

- Fianna                          www.rootsweb.ancestry.com/~fianna/
- Fáilte Romhat                   www.failteromhat.com
- Ireland Genealogy Links         www.genealogylinks.net/uk/ireland
- A Little Bit of Ireland         www.celticcousins.net/ireland
- The Irish Genealogical Project  www.igp-web.com
- The Irish Archives              www.theirisharchives.com

## Commercial websites

There are several popular commercial family history websites available which will occasionally be referenced in this book. These platforms offer many documentary resources which have been digitised and / or indexed in partnership with archives, libraries and societies in Ireland, the UK, and worldwide. Most will offer the option of a short trial subscription, and various subscription tiers should you wish to continue beyond that.

- Findmypast                      www.findmypast.co.uk
- Ancestry                        www.ancestry.co.uk
- MyHeritage                      www.myheritage.com
- Irish Newspaper Archives        www.irishnewsarchive.com
- British Newspaper Archive       www.britishnewspaperarchive.co.uk

In the case of Findmypast and Ancestry there are further localised platforms available on a worldwide basis, offering the same content – for example, **www.ancestry.com** is the US-hosted site for Ancestry, whilst Findmypast has a dedicated Irish platform at **www.findmypast.ie**.

Although not a commercial website, FamilySearch (**www.familysearch. org**) is another major repository offering free access to digitised records. Registration is required.

## Family history and local studies societies

There are several genealogical and historical societies in Ireland, with many offering useful online holdings and listings, as well as resource centres that can be visited. Organisationally, however, the island is fairly fragmented, with various independent societies falling under different umbrella groups.

- The Council of Irish Genealogical Organisations (**www.cigo.ie**) is an umbrella group which has several organisations amongst its membership, the details for which can be accessed in the 'Constituent Organisations' page.
- Established in 1990, the Genealogical Society of Ireland (**https:// familyhistory.ie**) has a dedicated research and archive centre, *An Daonchartlann*, based at Carlisle Pier in Dún Laoghaire.

- The North of Ireland Family History Society (**www.nifhs.org**) is the umbrella body for family history societies in Northern Ireland, with branches based in Ballymena, Belfast, Coleraine, Fermanagh, Foyle (Derry), Killyleagh, Larne, Lisburn, Newtownabbey, North Armagh (Portadown), North Down and Ards (Bangor), and Omagh. Some of the societies have their own websites, whilst others use the main umbrella site to advertise their activities. A dedicated research centre is based at Newtownabbey in County Antrim.
- The Ulster Historical Foundation, formed in 1956, is based in Newtownards, near Belfast, and has a considerably well-developed online presence at **www.ancestryireland.com**. The site offers a range of transcribed records on a commercial basis, but an interesting free offering is an app for Apple- or Android-based mobile devices, which accompanies a driving tour around 200 locations of interest to Ulster-Scots-based history. Its eBooks page also offers several downloadable publications, some for a fee and others free of charge. The Foundation has a substantial publications programme, with its own dedicated bookshop platform at **www.booksireland.org.uk**, including many essential tomes for research such as the *Ordnance Survey Memoirs* collection (p.144).

There are two main umbrella groups for local studies societies, these being the Federation for Ulster Local Studies Limited at **https://fuls.org.uk.uk** and the Federation of Local History Societies (*Conascadh na gCumann Staire Áitiúla*) at **https://localhistory.ie**. Each website links to member sites across Ireland, providing a great deal of useful resources for historical research.

## Professional genealogists

If you are unable to visit archive centres or libraries within the Republic of Ireland or Northern Ireland, professional genealogists may be able to assist. The following bodies provide listings for many offering their services:

- Association of Professional   **www.apgen.org**
  Genealogists
- Accredited Genealogists Ireland   **https://accreditedgenealogists.ie**
- Ancestor Network   **www.ancestornetwork.ie**
- Irish Family History Centre   **www.irishfamilyhistorycentre.com**

- Society of Genealogists of          **http://sgni.net**
  Northern Ireland
- Ulster Historical Foundation        **www.ancestryireland.com**

## Ye don't ask, ye don't get!

There will be many institutions that can help with your research, and many records across time documenting the existence of a place where your family was once based. But in the same way that distant cousins might be able to tell you a little about earlier generations of relatives, it is also worth remembering that many of the places that you are interested in actually still exist.

In 2020, I made a DNA connection with a very distant cousin with a farm property within the County Londonderry-based parish of Ballyrashane. Upon establishing contact it soon transpired that he was actually the owner of much of the same farmland as held by my direct ancestor 150 years ago, which had remained continually within the possession of that branch of the family. Not only did he share many stories with me about why land was divided, exchanged and passed on at various points in the past, he actually emailed me a link to some video footage filmed with a drone showing me the layout of the farm! Even if a property is no longer held by the family, the owner of a house where your family once resided may be interested enough to share information with you about it.

There is absolutely no obligation whatsoever for a property owner to allow you access to any information that they might hold concerning a property, but a polite letter outlining the reason for your interest in a holding may well be reciprocated with the same interest at the other end. In a restaurant in Brussels many years ago I told the waiter that one of my grandfathers had been born in the same building over a century ago, when it was a shoe shop occupied by my Scottish great-grandparents. The manager heard about it, and was so delighted with our story that not only did he allow my wife and I a brief visit to the first floor to see where my grandfather was born, he also provided us with a free bottle of wine.

The bottom line, as my mother always said, is that 'God loves a trier'.

If ye don't ask, ye don't get!

*Chapter 2*

# A BRIEF HISTORY OF IRELAND

For many centuries, the island of Ireland existed as a single country, but for much of that time it was a nation in constant turmoil politically. Often the cause for much of the conflict has been cited as religious in origin, and occasionally that has been true, but Ireland's historic pains go much further back in time to the first millennium, and are based on its core assets, its peoples and its land.

The following is a brief summary of the history of Ireland, to provide a backdrop to which the records for land and property research can be set against.

## Gaels, Vikings and the Old English

Much of the early history of the Irish is perhaps as often derived from myth as it is from historical evidence, but by the seventh century, Ireland was made up of many provincial Gaelic kingdoms.

In this early tribal period, inhabitants of various clans and septs lived within large kin-based groups known as fine. Amongst these were smaller kin-based groups of different extending degrees of relationships, defined as the *gelfine, derbfine, iarfine* and *indfine*. Although never a unified nation, these early Irish inhabitants did share the same culture and language, and adhered to a civil legal system known as 'Brehon Law', which had a major influence on the regulation of property and inheritance. With its laws of succession codified through the rules of 'tanistry' (*tanaisteacht* in Irish), a king or chief known as a 'toisech' would be succeeded by a deputy known as a 'tanist'. Early Ireland society did not exercise primogeniture, and so the tanist, who had previously been elected from close relatives within the derbfine (*dearbhfine* in Irish), was not necessarily a son of the present incumbent. From these ancient roles come the modern political offices in Ireland of *Taoiseach*, the Irish Prime Minister, and *Tánaiste*, the Deputy Prime Minister.

Norwegian Vikings first made their way towards Ireland in the late eighth century, and within the next two centuries had established urban settlements on the eastern and southern coasts, founding walled towns such as Dublin, Waterford, Wexford, Cork and Limerick. Although not overtly powerful, they were respected for their trading abilities and largely co-existed peacefully with the native Irish clans. They intermarried with their Irish neighbours, and their descendants, a mix of Norse and Gael, later became known as the *Ostmen* ('east men'), or to the Irish in their own language as the *Gall-ghaeil* (the 'foreign Gaels').

The Norman regime in England turned its attention towards Ireland in 1169, in response to a plea for assistance by the exiled Irish king of Leinster, Diarmait Mac Murchada (Murrough). Norman troops landed in Wexford, and the throne was soon reclaimed for the king. Mac Murchada granted the city of Wexford to leading Norman barons, as well as land between Wexford and Waterford. Richard de Clare, 2nd Earl of Pembroke (also known as Strongbow) was granted permission to marry the king's daughter Aoife and to become heir to his lands. Worried that a rival Norman kingdom could be established in Ireland, the king of England, Henry II, arrived in Ireland with his own army in 1171 to

*Reginald's Tower, Waterford, where Richard de Clare (Strongbow) married Aoife Mac Murchada in 1171. Although the current building dates back to the fourteenth century, it was built on the site of an earlier Danish fortification from 1003.*

take overlordship of its kings and bishops, which was duly accepted. From this point onwards, a steady stream of Norman settlers continued to make their way to Ireland to carve out territories for themselves.

The original Viking settlement at Dublin had soon become a Norman stronghold in an area known as 'the Pale'. To go beyond its borders risked a journey into the Gaelic heartlands not yet conquered, but many did so, and soon became integrated into the Gaelic lifestyle. Picking up the language, customs and mannerisms of those with whom they intermarried, and in some cases becoming more Irish than the Irish, to their posterity they were, nevertheless, still identified as outsiders by the term 'Old English'. Meanwhile in the north, there was a later separate incursion from Scotland in the fifteenth century, when Gaelic-speaking 'gallowglass' mercenaries from the Western Isles (from *gall óglaigh* in Gaelic, meaning foreign warriors), employed by the Earls of Ulster, took possession of parts of County Down and the Glens of Antrim.

### The Tudor Conquest

Following the English Reformation of the 1530s, a series of more carefully planned colonial plantations were attempted in Ireland by the English Crown. The first of these were carried out under the authority of the Protestant king Henry VIII, his Roman Catholic daughter Mary (and her husband, Philip II of Spain), and then her Protestant sister Elizabeth I. Lands were confiscated in counties Laois and Offaly, and an English settlement introduced. A similar colonisation attempt was made in the east of Ulster in the 1570s to try to prevent a further foothold being gained by Gaelic Scottish clans. Both attempts were largely unsuccessful.

Following rebellions against its rule in the 1580s, the English Crown again tried a plantation scheme in the province of Munster. Some 3,000 settlers were this time sent to defend a million acres of land, but they were dispossessed of their holdings during the Nine Years War of 1594–1603. This uprising against English rule was led by the Gaelic Irish chiefs Hugh O'Neill of Tyrone and Red Hugh O' Donnell of Tyrconnell, but collapsed in a military campaign in a retaliation that devastated much of Ireland.

In the peace that followed in the immediate aftermath, the first successful Scottish colonisation attempt was made by two lairds, Hugh Montgomery and James Hamilton. In return for assisting Con O'Neill to escape from Carrickfergus Castle and to secure a royal pardon after the murder of an English soldier, they managed to obtain a large portion of County Down and a small part of County Antrim, commencing a settlement there of Scots in 1606. This settlement was encouraged by the new 'British' Crown, following the recent convergence of the royal lines of Scotland and England at the Union of the Crowns in 1603. With Elizabeth I having died without an heir, the Scottish king James VI had been invited to take the throne of England, and in doing so became James I of Great Britain. Concerned that Ulster was still the thorniest part of Ireland to contend with, the new king soon grabbed an opportunity to launch the largest colonisation scheme yet by a British monarch.

## The Plantations of Ulster

On 4 September 1607, the Irish chiefs Hugh O' Neill and Rory O' Donnell, along with ninety followers, set sail for Spain in the hopes of raising an army with which to return to finish off the job they had started in their previous campaign. Their departure, known today as the 'Flight of the Earls', was immediately followed by their lands being declared by the Crown as forfeit. With the Hamilton-Montgomery settlements already established in Down, and the continued presence of Scots in the northern parts of Antrim, James implemented a new and massive plantation scheme to bring the rest of Ulster under his control.

Three-quarters of lands held by Irish landholders in the counties of Coleraine (now part of County Londonderry), Tyrconnell (now Donegal), Tyrone, Fermanagh, Armagh and Cavan were confiscated and distributed to Scots and English settlers, known as undertakers and servitors, as well as to some 'deserving Irish' inhabitants deemed to be loyal. The land was granted to the undertakers in 'fee simple' (outright ownership), which could then be parcelled out further by them to tenants in 'fee farm' (p.103).

To finance this 'Plantation of Ulster', The Honourable The Irish Society was formed in London, which in 1610 was given the town of Derry to develop, with work then commencing in 1613 to transform it into the first planned city in Ireland. To reflect the London livery companies' funding, it was re-named 'Londonderry' and granted a royal charter. Although some towns had been created in Ireland in the medieval period long before the Plantations, such as Carrickfergus, Downpatrick and Cavan, a further forty towns were granted charters of incorporation, half of them within Ulster, to help urbanise the country and to encourage trade (p.32). These newly incorporated towns could also send elected members to the Irish Parliament in Dublin.

Although the Scots were invited to participate, this project was very much based on the power of the English in Ireland, with Scotland still a distinct, independent nation from England. Scottish undertakers wishing to participate therefore had to seek letters of denization or grants of naturalisation from the Crown, to protect their property rights in Ireland as loyal subjects.

Religion had now also well and truly entered the mix. Those who came from England were adherents to the Anglican-based Church of England, whilst the Scots were largely devout Presbyterians. To establish Protestantism as the dominant religion in Ulster, the Anglican Church was handed the properties of the Roman Catholic Church. This was despite some 80 per cent of the settlers being Scottish Presbyterians, who worshipped through a very theologically different form of Protestantism, created from a separate Reformation in Scotland in 1560, and considered by the English to be 'dissenters'.

Nevertheless, the dramatic increase of towns sending elected Protestant members to the Irish Parliament in Dublin soon saw the Old English Catholic members becoming a minority.

## A war in three kingdoms

Despite the tolerance of the English and Scottish settlers in Ulster towards each other during the Plantation, back in Britain a line was about to be crossed that would stir up a hornets' nest. When James' son, Charles I, attempted to impose Anglicanism in Scotland, Presbyterians both there and in Ulster were infuriated. As the king set about raising an Irish Catholic army to attack the Scots if they refused to accept his new regime, the remnants of the old Gaelic order, still in possession of 60 per cent of their former lands, seized their chance. Under Phelim O'Neill and Rory O' More, a bloody rebellion was launched against the Protestant settlers. Some 12,000 were murdered and thousands more fled back to Britain, as a new 'Irish Catholic Confederation' sought to regain power across the island, whilst also remaining loyal to Charles I.

When news reached Charles I of the rebellion, he was asked by his Protestant subjects in Ireland to send over troops to defend them. Charles in turn requested that the Scottish Parliament do so, a body which which continued to distrust the monarch over his intentions to install Anglicanism in Scotland. They eventually agreed to the king's request only when he guaranteed that the venture would be paid for by the English Parliament. A Scottish Covenanting army arrived in Ireland in March 1642 and retaliated against the rebellion with a ferocious slaughter of Irish Catholics (a series of depositions detailing the atrocities have been made available online by Trinity College Dublin at **https://1641. tcd.ie**). Throughout the next decade, Britain and Ireland descended into the insanity of a civil war, which formed part of the much larger 'Wars of the Three Kingdoms'. The Catholic rebellion in Ireland was finally

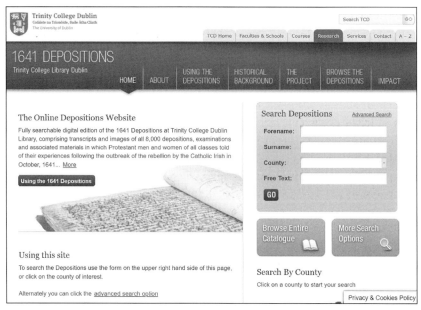

*The 1641 Depositions website from Trinity College Dublin.*

crushed by the Cromwellian conquest of 1649–53, which included the controversial massacre of Catholic Confederate and English Royalist troops, as well as many civilians, at the Siege of Drogheda in 1649.

Oliver Cromwell's settlement led to Catholic-owned lands being confiscated and redistributed to loyal English settlers (p.83), and Catholics were banned from holding office in the Irish Parliament. In the subsequent redistribution of the seized territories to the settlers, many Scottish Presbyterians found themselves equally discriminated against by an unforgiving English Commonwealth, with lands only granted to English settlers. Despite Presbyterian support for William of Orange in the later Williamite Wars against James II from 1689 to 1691, as part of the so-called 'Glorious Revolution', the Scots and their descendants remained second-class citizens, despite forming the majority of the colonist population. A series of 'Penal Laws' passed against them and Irish Catholics became so intolerable that many of the Presbyterians set sail for the American colonies in the 1700s, where, being known as the Scotch-Irish, they would ultimately form a significant fighting contingent against the British Crown during the Revolutionary War of the late 1770s.

For the majority Catholic population, the Penal Laws were relentless. In terms of land ownership, for example, Catholics were banned from purchasing leases under thirty-one years, they could not inherit land from a Protestant, and their own land was to be divided equally amongst all sons after death, unless the eldest son had converted to Protestantism.

**Rebellion, union and more rebellion**

Common cause was soon found between the disaffected Ulster-based Scottish descended Presbyterians and their Roman Catholic neighbours from across the island. Together they launched a rebellion across the island in 1798 to overthrow a Dublin government perceived by now to consist of self-serving Anglo-Irish aristocrats. When this rising by the United Irishmen was crushed, the British Parliament resolved to solve its 'Irish question' by assimilating Ireland in 1801 into a newly expanded 'United Kingdom of Great Britain and Ireland' – not least for strategic reasons, with the rebels having previously been aided by England's great enemy, the French.

Although some in this Anglo-Irish dominated society went on to prosper within the UK and its associated worldwide empire, the union was an uneasy solution, and it was not long before further uprisings were attempted against British control.

In 1848, the Young Irelanders launched the first major attempt. Whilst the potato crop, the food of the poor, had failed because of blight, a surplus of grain and livestock was being exported overseas from Ireland under armed military escort, showing the inability, and as some saw it, the unwillingness, of Westminster to help those starving in their country. The authorities got wind of their movement and quelled the uprising before it had gained much traction.

A decade later, in 1858, the Irish Republican Brotherhood (IRB) was established by a former Young Irelander called James Stephens, in tandem with an American organisation called the Fenian Brotherhood, but another planned insurrection in 1867 was similarly intercepted, with many arrests.

**The Land War and reform**

Throughout the 1870s and 1880s, the main issue of the day was land reform, which soon became tied to the notion of self-government for Ireland. The Home Rule League, set up by a Protestant barrister called Isaac Butt in 1873, managed to get fifty-nine MPs, Protestant and Catholic, to Westminster, but was initially hampered procedurally by hostile parliamentary opponents. As Charles Stewart Parnell took over the reins, this dramatically changed, with Parnell's dynamic leadership soon attracting support from many, including the IRB.

When agricultural prices in Ireland crashed in 1878, thousands of destitute tenants were ruthlessly evicted from their homes, with no recourse for appeal. So desperate was the plight of tenants in the west and south that from 1879 to 1882 there followed a 'Land War' with much violence across the country. Parnell set up the Irish National Land

League in 1879, which was soon accused of orchestrating the violence. Its members, including Parnell, were arrested and imprisoned, but the Liberal Prime Minister, William Gladstone, knew that reforms were urgently needed. An Act was granted in 1881 to give tenants the right of redress through an Irish Land Commission, and Parnell was freed (for more on the Irish Land Acts, see Chapter 6).

Realising that Irish self-government was fast becoming a logical necessity, Gladstone introduced a Home Rule bill in 1885, but this was defeated in the House of Commons by many within his own party, as well as by Irish Unionists. A further Home Rule bill in 1893 was similarly defeated. In 1910, the Liberal government, depending on the support of the devolution-seeking Irish Parliamentary Party, finally managed to pass a third Home Rule bill, despite the creation of an armed resistance movement to the measure, the Ulster Volunteer Force, and an opposing and parallel Irish Volunteers drawn up in the south (heavily infiltrated by the IRB) in favour of it. All out civil war over the issue was only averted with the outbreak of the First World War, when the Liberals agreed to postpone the implementation of Home Rule, and only after significant amendments to appease the northern Unionists.

Whilst the war provided a temporary and uneasy truce between members of the opposing militias, with both now offering to fight for

*The General Post Office in Dublin, from where the Irish Republic was proclaimed at the Easter Rising of 1916.*

Britain in the belief that they would afterwards be suitably rewarded politically, a small core within the Irish Volunteers and other republican groups saw 'England's difficulty as Ireland's opportunity'. With the UK distracted in Europe, at Easter 1916 they initiated a rebellion to establish an Irish republic, independent of British rule, seizing control of key institutions in Dublin, in an event which became known as the Easter Rising. The rebels held out for a week, but were ultimately defeated, and its leaders were executed as traitors.

Whilst the rebellion failed in its immediate aims, the wave of revulsion caused by the prisoners' treatment politically energised the recently created party, Sinn Féin (which, despite popular belief, actually had little involvement with the Rising), as did efforts to introduce conscription in Ireland to the British Army in 1918. Sinn Féin scored a landslide victory in parliamentary elections in December, and on 21 January 1919, established itself as the first Irish Parliament, *Dáil Éireann*, in what would be one of many opening acts in a new 'War of Independence' against British rule.

## The partitioned island

In May 1921, the entire island was partitioned by a now desperate British government into two separate states, following the enactment of the Government of Ireland Act 1920. The Act stipulated that:

> Northern Ireland shall consist of the parliamentary counties of Antrim, Armagh, Down, Fermanagh, Londonderry and Tyrone, and the parliamentary boroughs of Belfast and Londonderry, and Southern Ireland shall consist of so much of Ireland as is not comprised within the said parliamentary counties and boroughs.

The new Northern Irish government soon established a parliament, but the equivalent body envisaged under the Act for Southern Ireland never met, with Sinn Féin's Dáil instead continuing to meet.

In December 1922, the southern counties left the United Kingdom altogether to become the Irish Free State (*Saorstat Éireann*), but a split in Sinn Féin over the Treaty conceded by the British for its establishment, which omitted Northern Ireland from its jurisdiction, led to the brief and tragic Irish Civil War from 1922 to 1923, in which the pro-Treaty faction won.

Although nominally independent, the Free State still remained as a dominion of the British Crown, and was subject to Treaty obligations with Britain, allowing, for example, the use of Irish ports by the Royal Navy.

A Boundary Commission established as part of the Anglo-Irish Treaty of 1921, designed to review whether there should be any adjustment to the border as initially drawn, met in 1924, and proposed an exchange of some border regions between the north and the south, with the south to gain a net area of some 200 square miles, but the Commission was disbanded in late 1925, its recommendations not accepted.

In 1937, a new Constitution of Ireland was implemented in the south, with the Free State named officially as Ireland (*Éire*), and establishing itself as a republic in all but name. With the passing of the Republic of Ireland Act 1948, from 1949 Ireland's southern twenty-six counties finally completed their journey towards full independence from the UK.

## Terminology

Within this book, I will refer to 'Ireland' when I specifically mean the name of the island or the pre-1921 country of that name. For post-Partition discussion, and for contemporary references, I will refer to the 'Republic of Ireland' to mean the southern twenty-six counties (or the 'Free State' if required in context) and 'Northern Ireland' to refer to the north-eastern six counties, reserving the word 'Ulster' for the nine-county province of that name. I am not a constitutional lawyer, just a humble genealogist trying to get by in life, so no offence is meant from such terms, if sought!

So this is the backdrop. Throughout all of these momentous events, our ancestors worked, raised families, worshipped, fought for their rights, and defended their respective traditional communities. Now let us take a look at where they once lived, starting with the infrastructure of Ireland itself, and the various administrative boundaries that emerged within it across time, through which the island's various rulers governed.

*Chapter 3*

# BOUNDARIES AND ADMINISTRATION

Acurse of Irish genealogy often encountered by those with family who emigrated, is the simple description of a family member having been 'born Ireland' to indicate origins in the Emerald Isle.

To be frank, this can be about as useful as a hole in a doughnut. For such a small island, Ireland is still a fairly big place, and if your ancestors fall into this category, it is often the case that you may need to do more work first within the country to which they emigrated, to find additional records there to help pinpoint a more specific place of origin.

If you are lucky, you may find a bit more detail about where in Ireland they hailed from. How such a place of origin is recorded, however, may well fall under one of many different administrative region descriptions for the area from which your ancestor hailed – and it may not be immediately obvious from the place name that you have what type of region it is that it is actually referring to.

There were, and still are, many types of administrative land divisions created in Ireland over the centuries, both for religious reasons and for legal purposes such as taxation, elections and probate. A highly recommended guide for your family history library, which provides maps depicting the most important historic administrative divisions on the island, is the second edition of Brian Mitchell's excellent book *A New Genealogical Atlas of Ireland* (see p.150). Many online finding aids also exist to help locate areas and to understand the various geographical territories to which it may have formed a part, which will be noted in this chapter.

But let us start with the basics – what exactly is Ireland in geographical terms, and how has it been historically carved up?

## The island of Ireland

The name of Ireland in Irish Gaelic is *Éire* (also *Èirinn* in Scottish Gaelic, and *Nerin* in Manx), which is believed to trace its etymology back to the name of a previously worshipped goddess in ancient times known as *Ériu*. In the second century AD, Claudius Ptolemy described the island as *Iouernia*, whilst in Latin the Romans called it *Hibernia*.

The constitutional evolution of Ireland into the two modern territories of 'Northern Ireland' and 'Ireland' ('Republic of Ireland') is discussed in Chapter 2

## Provinces and counties

For much of Ireland's existence there have been four historic provinces, being Ulster, Munster, Leinster and Connacht. Prior to the arrival of the Normans in 1169 there was in fact a fifth, with the province or kingdom of Meath constituting much of the northern half of what is now Leinster. The Irish word for a province, *cúige*, derives from this period (*cúig* means 'five' in Irish). The existence of various small provinces fluctuated after

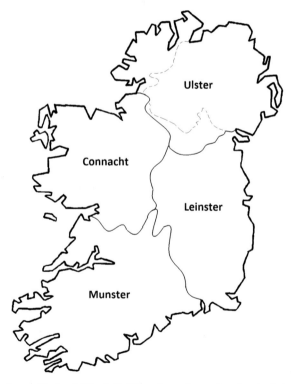

*The four provinces of Ireland. The dotted line shows the modern border between Northern Ireland and the Republic of Ireland.*

*The thirty-two historic counties of Ireland.*

the arrival of the Normans, but in 1610 their number and boundaries were permanently set by James I of Great Britain to the four that we are familiar with today.

The four provinces were gradually subdivided into counties following the Norman invasion, for taxation and judicial purposes, with lands drawn together from more ancient tribal territorial designations in a process of 'shiring', as had been carried out in England. Different parts of the island were shired at different times, with Ulster the last province to be so carved up.

For most of our period of interest in this book there have existed thirty-two counties, and their importance today is as much to do with sport as it has been historically for governance. It would be remiss of me at this point not to note my father-in-law's lifelong devotion to his native Tipperary (*'Up Tipp!'*), and my wife's continuing insistence that she is a Kilkenny Cat.

Remember that the thirty-two historic counties of Ireland remain just that – historic counties. Following the Local Government (Ireland) Act of 1898, Ireland's counties were reconstituted as administrative counties, and these remained in government use both north and south beyond Partition, in Northern Ireland until 1973 and in the Republic until 2002.

The four historic provinces of Ireland are constituted as follows:

### i) Province of Ulster / *Cúige Uladh*

Counties: Antrim, Armagh, Cavan, Donegal, Down, Fermanagh, Londonderry, Monaghan, Tyrone.

Donegal was previously part of a larger county called Tyrconnell (which also included small parts of Sligo, Fermanagh and Londonderry), and from 1922 to 1927 was briefly designated by its own county council by the name of Tirconaill. The county of Londonderry was created during the Plantation of Ulster (p.20), replacing the smaller county of Coleraine, with lands appended from Antrim, Tyrone and Tyrconnell. The city of the same name was in fact previously based in territory controlled as part of Tyrconnell, prior to the creation of the new county.

Upon Partition in 1921, it should be noted that it was not just Ireland which was divided but also the province of Ulster, with counties Cavan, Donegal and Monaghan joining the twenty-three other counties within Leinster, Connacht and Munster to form the Free State, and later the Republic.

### ii) Province of Munster / *Cúige Mumhan*

Counties: Clare, Cork, Kerry, Limerick, Tipperary and Waterford.

Located to the south of the island, Munster's cities of Cork, Limerick and Waterford were all founded as settlements by Norse Vikings. The province's flag denotes three crowns, representing the earlier Gaelic kingdoms of Desmond, Thomond and Ormond.

The county of Tipperary historically held *palatine* status, which operated with a great deal of independence from the Crown, but the County Palatine of Tipperary Act of 1715 stripped the county of its rights following the flight of the 2nd Duke of Ormonde, James Butler, who was accused of being a traitor with Jacobite sympathies.

During the Irish Civil War of 1922–3 a great deal of activity occurred in Munster, with strong support for the anti-Treaty side.

### iii) Province of Leinster / *Cúige Laighean*

Counties: Carlow, Dublin, Kildare, Kilkenny, Laois, Longford, Louth, Meath, Offaly, Westmeath, Wexford and Wicklow.

Laois, also noted historically as Leix, was initially known from its shiring in the Tudor plantation of 1556 as Queen's County, and Offaly as King's County, named for England's Catholic Queen Mary I, and her husband, King Philip II of Spain. These names were fixed in statute by the Local Government (Ireland) Act of 1898.

Following the formation of the Irish Free State in 1922, the names of the counties were changed back to Laois and Offaly on an informal basis. There has never been an Act of the Irish Parliament to repeal the designation from 1898, and as such, any transactions to this day concerning land and property in the two counties may still reference them as being within Queen's County or King's County.

### iv) Province of Connacht / *Cúige Chonnacht*
Counties: Galway, Leitrim, Mayo, Roscommon and Sligo.

Historically also noted as Connaught, the name of this province is derived from the *Connachta*, the supposed descendants of the mythical High King Conn of the Hundred Battles.

Today, Connacht hosts the largest *gaeltacht* (Irish-speaking) region in Ireland, based in Counties Galway and Mayo, including the Aran Islands and Connemara.

### Counties corporate and county boroughs
In addition to the historic counties, there were also several 'counties corporate' created prior to the early nineteenth century, which were essentially several of the larger towns and cities re-designated with county status. One of these was Carrickfergus, the County Antrim-based town in which I grew up as a child, which was a county corporate from the early fourteenth century until 1898, at which point it was then incorporated into the wider administrative county of Antrim. Others in existence included Cork, Drogheda, Dublin, Galway, Kilkenny, Limerick, Londonderry and Waterford.

From 1898, some of the counties corporate were reconstituted as county boroughs, with continuing independent administrative functions to their surrounding counties. These were Carrickfergus, Cork, Dublin, Limerick, Londonderry and Waterford. Galway briefly joined the list in 1986, but in the Republic county boroughs were eventually abolished in 2001. The Northern Irish counties boroughs ceased to be constituted as such from 1973.

Today, Northern Ireland now utilises eleven local government districts, whilst in the Republic there are thirty-one local authorities, comprised mainly of county councils, but also including city and county councils, and city councils.

## Boroughs and charter towns

Following the Norman invasion of Ireland and the establishment of the Old English settlers (p.19), a series of self-contained towns were created by Crown charters with municipal borough status, predominantly in Munster and Leinster. They were effectively granted the means of self-governance from the local counties and provided an exclusive right for merchants and craftsmen to trade within their walled confines. Over 170 were created, but not all survived.

To be able to work in a borough, a merchant or a craftsman had to first become a 'burgess' or 'freeman', a right that could be inherited, obtained through marriage of a burgess' daughter, or gained upon the completion of an apprenticeship to a burgess or freeman. This had the effect of keeping the control of the governance of such jurisdictions within the hands of a small number of locally powerful families over several generations. In addition to their domestic duties, boroughs also had the right to send elected representatives to participate in the national Irish Parliament.

In the early 1600s, a further series of boroughs or charter towns were created in Ulster as part of the Plantation (p.20), with Belfast perhaps the most significant. Each settlement involved was granted a charter of incorporation to create market towns and fairs, and to permit guilds and trade incorporations to be established to promote a local urbanised economy.

A useful article on the impact of James I's new boroughs was published in *History Ireland*, Volume 21 (March/April 2013), available online at **https://web.archive.org/web/20201125111813/www.historyireland.com/early-modern-history-1500-1700/the-greatest-gerrymander-in-irish-history-james-is-40-boroughs-of-1612-13.**

A guide and map, *The Charter Towns of Ulster 1613–2013*, can be purchased from the Ulster Historical Foundation (p.15).

## Baronies and civil parishes

There were historically well over 300 baronies in Ireland, which are mostly formed as subdivisions of counties following the English Tudor conquest of the country from 1530 onwards. Some of the earlier baronies were later divided into half-baronies, whilst others merged. A useful list is found online at **https://en.wikipedia.org/wiki/List_of_baronies_of_Ireland**.

Baronies served several administrative purposes. During the various sixteenth- and seventeenth-century-based plantation schemes in Ireland, for example, the colonists were settled by barony, whilst taxes to provide

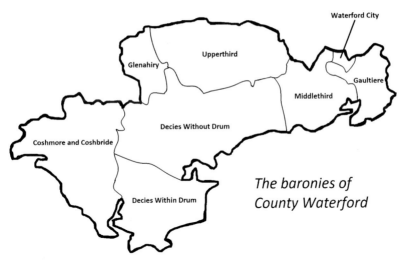

*The historic baronies of County Waterford in the province of Munster.*

for public works were set at rates per barony. The decennial censuses (p.49) from 1821 to 1891 were recorded by barony, before District Electoral Divisions (p.36) were utilised.

However, as further administrative units were developed in the nineteenth century the barony became increasingly more obsolete. They eventually lost most administrative functions in 1898, although you will find some records still collated after this by the barony within which they were recorded – for example, the post-1908 Old Age Pension applications for the north (p.51), held at PRONI, are found in large bound volumes collated by the name of the barony.

Baronies can usually be subdivided into civil parishes. They were used for taxation purposes, and as administration districts you will find these regularly noted in records such as census returns, although they became increasingly less important following the introduction of poor law unions (p.36) in the nineteenth century.

Prior to the disestablishment of the Church of Ireland in 1871, the names of civil parishes and their boundaries shared those of the Anglican parishes. Civil parishes were also abolished from 1898 as an official boundary measurement for administration purposes.

Useful civil parish maps for individual counties are available via **www.johngrenham.com/places/civil_index.php**.

### Townlands

Civil parishes can be further subdivided into areas called townlands, which are by far perhaps the most important administrative areas that you will need to identify for your ancestral research. You may think that you have cracked it when you discover that your ancestor was called Michael Murray and that he came from a particular parish – but that joy may be short-lived when you then discover that there were some thirty townlands within that parish, with a Michael Murray in each one!

Townlands were a land unit long in use before the Normans came, and continue to be important to this day, particularly in rural areas. In the province of Ulster they were more anciently known as 'ballyboes', from the Gaelic words *baile bó*, denoting the amount of land needed to graze a cow. Other words that can be found to denote townlands in Ireland include 'tates' and 'polls', which are sometimes included in the names of the areas concerned, e.g. Ballintate in County Armagh, and Poulawillin in County Clare.

There have been more than 60,000 townlands noted as existing across Ireland. The average size is just over 300 acres, however, some are considerably smaller at just a few acres, whilst the largest is over 7,000 acres. In the 1830s, the boundaries of townlands were standardised as part of the work of the Ordnance Survey (p.142).

Confusingly, several townlands may exist with the same name. On the first page of the *Townlands Index* from 1861 (p.38), for example, there are four townlands noted by the name of Abbey, with one located in County Cork, one in County Leitrim, and two within County Galway (in separate baronies). There are also twenty-one Abbeylands, including variants such as Abbey-lands, Abbey Land, and Abbeyland Little. This is why the name of the civil parish and even the barony can often be equally crucial when trying to target a location.

Bear in mind also that some townlands may have had more than one name. Within the twenty-one Abbeylands mentioned above, for example, one is noted as 'Abbeyland and Charlestown or Ballnamonster'. And whilst the indexes are fairly thorough, occasionally some old townland names may slip through. An interesting example I came across within my own research concerned a townland named Ballyvoy, as identified in several records located. The family in question had been based near the village of Doagh in the County Antrim parish of Templepatrick, and yet every townland guide I consulted stated that Ballyvoy was located in the parish of Culfeightrin on the northern coast. This made no sense whatsoever, and so I kept digging. It was not until I located an advert within the *Belfast Newsletter* from 13 January 1893 that I finally worked out where it was. In this newspaper I found an advert for the sale of a freehold property, which identified it as:

All that valuable farm of land and premises, in the townland of Ballyvoy, also known as Duncansland.

And further on within the advert:

> The Lands are all arable, well fenced, drained, and watered, and are situate in one of the best farming districts in County Antrim, about two miles from the Village of Doagh, on the leading road to Ballymena.

At long last I had located it – Duncansland made perfect sense, and yet although named as such in the townland indexes, its alternative name of Ballyvoy makes no appearance at all in any of them.

The use of townlands was abandoned for postal purposes by the Royal Mail in Northern Ireland in the 1970s, with the use of postcodes in the north being deemed sufficient alongside street addresses. Despite this, many campaigns are now seeing the reintroduction of townland names to signs denoting street addresses, in a bid to help preserve their contribution to the local heritage.

In the Republic of Ireland, townlands continue to be used in addresses for folk in rural areas, although a new Eircode postcode system was introduced in 2014 to make it easier for deliveries, with people often spelling individual townland names differently. Each Eircode has seven characters, with the first three referring to a town or townland, and the remaining characters forming what is known as a 'unique identifier' for a specific address.

Undoubtedly both postcodes and Eircodes will help to target the mail a little better for all in the future, but it remains a fact of life that there is not a lot of poetry to be found within them.

## Other historic land divisions

There are many other historic land units that you might come across including 'ballybetaghs', 'quarters', 'seisreagh', 'sessiaghs', 'cartrons', and 'gneeves'.

To give an example, the following is a description on how land measurement was reckoned in parts of the province of Connacht, as described within the introduction to the seventeenth-century *Mayo Book of Survey and Distribution* (p.83):

> Former land measures, specified mostly by the main text, are Quarters, Cartrons and Gneeves; there are a few instances of Trines… As regards this last, indicating a third part, it enters into numerous place-names in the baronies of Costello, Murrish, Gallen and Tirawley… This land measure does not appear in either Reeves or in Larcom's Carew Ms. The latter states 'In Connoght all [land

measures] are called Quarters and Cartrons. A Quarter contains 4 cartrons, every cartron 30 acres.' According to Reeves... 'In Connaught the prevailing distribution was into townlands of vague inport; quarters the fourth part of the former; cartron the fourth of a quarter; gneeve the sixth of a quarter. The cartron was computed at 30 native acres'.

Such terms could mean different things in different parts of the country; if you come across them, you may need to consult more localised reference material to understand their full context.

## Poor Law Unions and District Electoral Divisions

The following top-down hierarchy describes the basic civil administrative divisions across the island prior to the twentieth century that you will need to know in particular for most areas of Irish research:

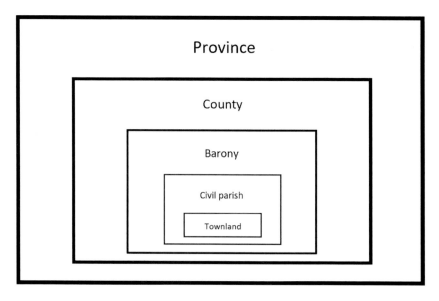

This is not quite a perfect description because there will be a few areas where territories may protrude from borders you may have expected them to remain within, but it holds for the majority of the island.

Of course, in Irish family history, it is often true that there is no gain without pain, so let us now look at how the state decided in nineteenth-century Ireland that it was getting a little bored with all of that, and instead tried something else.

In July 1838, an 'Act for the more effectual Relief of the Destitute Poor in Ireland' was passed, better known as the Poor Relief Act. Enacted partly as a measure to deter Irish emigration to Britain following the union of 1801, it set about the establishment of a new administrative system to enable the raising of taxation for the relief of the poor. The country was carved up into a series of Poor Law Unions (PLUs) with borders drawn up by the Poor Law Boundary Commission. These new PLUs had no respect for county or parish lines, and instead existed in parallel alongside them. A workhouse was established in each union, and a poor rate established as a new form of taxation to fund the system. Ireland was initially carved up into 130 unions, but this was extended to 163 by the end of 1850.

Just for good measure, these new PLUs were subdivided into a series of District Electoral Divisions (DEDs) for the election of Boards of Guardians to run the poor law unions. Initially there were 2,049 such divisions, but with the expansion of the number of poor law unions by 1850, this had increased to 3,438. From 1898 onwards, DEDs were also used as a basis for the election of officials to county, urban and district councils, with many subsequent changes to their boundaries. You will also note their use prominently within the 1901 and 1911 censuses (p.54).

In 1898, poor law unions finally replaced the civil parish and barony altogether as the main administrative unit across the country. Their use continued in the Republic of Ireland until 1925, at which point Boards of Guardians were replaced by county boards of health and public assistance, and in Northern Ireland until 1948, with the implementation of the new National Health Service.

For more on the creation of the poor law system in Ireland visit Peter Higginbotham's site at **www.workhouses.org.uk/Ireland** and an article by Dr Raymond Gillespie at **www.askaboutireland.ie/reading-room/ history-heritage/poor-law-union/poor-law-unions-and-their/index.xml**.

## Civil registration

From 1845, and later in 1864, the areas in which births, marriages and deaths were registered by the state through the new civil registration system (p.45) were designated as Superintendent Registrars Districts (SRDs), and based on the boundaries of the poor law unions first established in 1838. These were further subdivided into 720 Registrar's Districts or Dispensary Districts (for medical dispensation needs). Registration of the vital events was carried out locally, with returns sent regularly to the relevant SRD, and copies returned to the General Register Office (GRO) in Dublin. Following the Partition of Ireland (p.25), a separate GRO was established in Belfast to cater for registration in Counties Antrim, Down, Armagh, Fermanagh, Tyrone and Londonderry, whilst the GRO in Dublin continued to administer to the remaining counties beyond Northern Ireland.

As with the poor law unions, these registration districts did not cover the same areas as parishes, and you may find they cross parish, barony and even county boundaries. In my ancestral tree, for example, I have many events for relatives registered at the Registrar's District of Raphoe in County Donegal. This was part of the larger Superintendent Registrar's District of Strabane, which covered parts of both Counties Donegal and Tyrone.

A list of Superintendent Registrar's Districts can be found on Claire Santry's Irish Genealogy Toolkit site at **www.irish-genealogy-toolkit. com/Ireland-civil-registration.html**, whilst Shane Wilson's Registration District Map Browse tool at **www.swilson.info/regdistmap.php** can help to locate the names and locations of the relevant Registrar's Districts or Dispensary Districts within each SRD, as well as the names of adjacent districts in neighbouring SRDs.

A fairly detailed history of the Irish civil registration system, previously hosted on the old GRO Ireland website, has been cached by the Internet Archive's Wayback Machine at **https://tinyurl.com/GROirelandhistory**.

## Converting administrative units

If you have the name of a townland, or a civil parish, barony, county, poor law union or registration district, you may wish to find the names of the corresponding administrative units, which may have very different designations. Fortunately there is an ever growing number of tools available to help with the task.

Indexes to the names of townlands, civil parishes, baronies and poor law unions have been published on several occasions to tie in with the decennial censuses (p.49). In 1861, the *General Alphabetical Index to the Townlands and Towns, Parishes and Baronies of Ireland* was first published from the information collated from the 1851 census. It has been reprinted regularly by the Genealogical Publishing Company between 1984 and 2006, with separate indexes to townlands, parishes and indexes in Ireland, with each entry handily providing details of the Ordnance Survey map sheet on which the area of interest will be found. A more basic database offering information from this work, allowing you to convert from one administrative unit to another, is available in the IreAtlas Townlands Database at **https://thecore.com/seanruad**.

The exercise was repeated for the 1871 census with a publication in 1877 entitled *Alphabetical Index to the Townlands and Towns of Ireland*, which has been digitised by the University of Southampton and placed on the

Documenting Ireland: Parliament, People and Migration (DIPPAM) website at **www.dippam.ac.uk/eppi/documents/16380/page/433940**. Much of the same publication is also available from the University of Essex's Online Historical Population Reports (Histpop) website at **https://tinyurl.com/nba2ct7**.

More recently, the *General Topographical Index Consisting Of An Alphabetical Index Of The Townlands And Towns Of Ireland* was published in 1904 by the Commissioners of Census, drawing its list of townlands from the 1901 census. It has been made freely available in a searchable database format by the Irish Genealogical Research Society at **www.irishancestors. ie/resources/unique-resources/index-of-townlands-1901**.

Shane Wilson's Townland Search and Explorer facility at **www. swilson.info/explorerb.php** allows users to type in the name of a townland or town, and to then identify its associated administrative territories. Just for good measure, a result also identifies the number of acres contained within that townland. Handily, the site allows you to use wildcards * within your searches to replace possible missing letters if you are unsure of the spelling of a townland, or can only identify part of the spelling from a document with any confidence.

If I search on Shane's site for a townland beginning with Maghera, for example, using the wildcard (i.e. Maghera*), 176 possibilities are returned, broken down by county, poor law union, barony and parish. The tool can also be used in reverse to help determine the names of associated townlands, parishes, baronies, poor law unions and counties

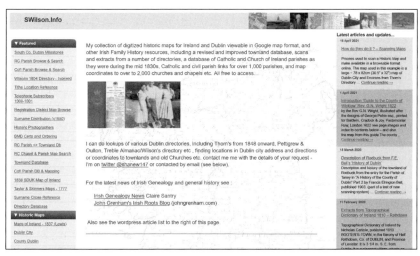

*Shane Wilson's useful website offers a variety of conversion tools to determine administrative units.*

for a specific area, by selecting the relevant area in drop-down menus for each administrative division.

The Ordnance Survey of Ireland's National Townland and Historical Map Viewer, freely accessible via **www.osi.ie/products/professional-mapping/historical-mapping/**, includes the Historic 6-inch First Edition OS map for Ireland (1829–41) in colour, with individual townland boundaries identified in red. These same maps were used for the various national valuation exercises carried out by Richard Griffith (p.90) and his team in the mid-nineteenth century.

The boundaries of townlands across Ireland can also be identified on the **www.townlands.ie** platform, although the returned maps will frustratingly only pinpoint the boundaries of the townland asked for, and not show those adjacent, which can be useful for research purposes. Boundary maps for Northern Irish townlands can be found at **www.placenamesni.org**.

### Religious parishes, dioceses and ecclesiastical provinces

The Church of Ireland, the state church from 1536 to 1869, had ecclesiastical parishes across the island which broadly shared the same boundaries as those of the civil parishes.

By contrast, the Roman Catholic Church's parishes have very different boundaries, albeit still based on the old civil parish system. In rural areas, many Catholic parishes were formed by an amalgamation of several civil parishes, whilst in other areas, large civil parishes may have been divided into smaller Catholic parishes. Just for good measure, there is quite often very little connection between the names of a civil or Anglican parish and the Roman Catholic parish covering the same area – a townland can exist in a civil parish and a Roman Catholic parish with two very different names. The boundaries of Roman Catholic parishes can be identified on the National Library of Ireland's Catholic Registers at the NLI platform at **https://registers.nli.ie**.

Both the Roman Catholic Church and the Church of Ireland are episcopal in nature, with the parishes historically enjoying oversight by bishops, through a higher administrative unit denoted as the diocese. The Roman Catholic Church is structured around twenty-six dioceses across Ireland, each with a bishop, who are in turn overseen by archbishops within the four ecclesiastical provinces of Armagh, Cashel, Dublin and Tuam. Within the Church of Ireland there are today twelve dioceses with bishops overseen by archbishops within the two episcopal provinces of Armagh and Dublin.

For the other major religion on the island, Presbyterianism, there was no parish system, unlike in Scotland from whence it originated.

Churches or 'meeting houses' were simply erected in an area where a congregational need was established, and these in term would subscribe to presbyteries and then synods of varying Presbyterian flavours.

For more on the structures of Presbyterian governance in Ireland, consult William Rouslton's *Researching Your Presbyterian Ancestors in Ireland* (Ulster Historical Foundation, 2020). Further details about the structures of its parent Scottish Kirk can be found in my book *Tracing Your Scottish Ancestors Through Church and State Records* (Pen and Sword, 2020).

## Manors and demesnes

Although the Normans had previously tried to introduce the feudal manor system into Ireland from 1170, with some notable success in particular in the north-east, east and south of the country, this original set up had been substantially reduced by the fifteenth and sixteenth centuries.

Under the feudal system, great landowners were granted charters that allowed them to establish manors on their lands, each with their own courts (known as the 'court baron' and the 'court leet') for administrative purposes, including the granting of leases to sub-tenants. The core part of the manor, in which the landowner resided as the lord of the manor, was known as the demesne (pronounced 'de-mains'), which he held from his feudal superior, i.e. the Crown, so long as he behaved himself and paid his relevant feudal obligations (financial payments or military service) when required. The rest of the manor was given over to the settlement of tenants, both free (known as 'gavillers') and unfree (the 'betaghs'), and for agriculture.

Sadly very few relevant records have survived for the medieval period, but a useful article on medieval manorial tenure can be found at **https://web.archive.org/web/20210331133036/http://what-when-how. com/medieval-ireland/manorialism-medieval-ireland/**.

For more on manorial records see p.116.

## Grand Juries

From Anglo-Norman times until the introduction of county councils in 1898, 'Grand Juries' acted as the main administrative arm of local government, meeting twice a year at the spring and autumn assizes, and at 'quarter sessions' four times a year.

Grand Juries were tasked not only with judicial functions but with facilitating public works in their locales, such as road and bridge repairs, the maintenance of gaols and hospitals, and setting local taxes such as the county cess. They consisted of between twelve and twenty-three volunteer jurors and were appointed by the High Sheriff for the county mainly from the landlord class (but not from the aristocracy), with Roman Catholics excluded from membership until 1793. Much of the communications infrastructure of Ireland exists today as a result of their early efforts, but being drawn largely from the landlord class, the juries were deeply unpopular in parts of the country.

Amongst the records that may be of interest, where they have survived, are published Grand Jury presentment and query books, which were produced from the end of the eighteenth century. These note lists of jurors appointed in each county, and in some cases high constables and sub constables (responsible for processes at the baronial level), as well as details of works to be carried out in the county, and the costs.

For example, the following is from the Grand Jury Query Book for the spring assizes at County Louth in 1824:

| No. | | £. | s. | d. |
|---|---|---|---|---|
| 444 | 8l. to Robert and John Balmer, to repair 40 perches of the road from Dundalk to Newry, by Rosskea, between Henry Boles' house in Roskea and Peter Crilly's house in Carrickedmond 21 feet wide and 16 with gravel, at 4s. per perch, 4s. 4d. stamp duty and 8s. wages – No. 17 | 3 | 17 | 10 |

The administrative powers of Grand Juries were stripped away from 1898, but they continued to meet at the assizes in a judicial capacity. Following Partition in 1922, they were abolished altogether in the Free State but continued to meet in Northern Ireland until their abolition in 1969.

Grand Jury records are available in many archives, with some collections online, including the 'Donegal, Grand Jury Presentments 1753–1899' collection on Findmypast (p.14), and the 'Louth Grand Jury Query Books (1786–1813, 1815–1816, 1823–1899)' collection on the Louth County Archives Service website at **www.louthcoco.ie/en/services/archives**.

A detailed list of surviving Grand Jury records for Ulster's nine counties is included in William Roulston's book (p.66). Further information on the records can also be found in *People, Place and Power: The Grand Jury System in Ireland* (Brian Gurrin, Trinity College Dublin, 2021), which can be found on the Beyond 2022 platform at **https://beyond2022.ie/the-grand-jury-system-in-ireland**.

# DISCOVER MORE ABOUT PEN & SWORD BOOKS

**Pen & Sword Books** have over 4000 books currently available, our imprints include: Aviation, Naval, Military, Archaeology, Transport, Frontline, Seaforth and the Battleground series, and we cover all periods of history on land, sea and air.

Can we stay in touch? From time to time we'd like to send you our latest catalogues, promotions and special offers by post. If you would prefer not to receive these, please tick this box. ☐

**We also think you'd enjoy some of the latest products and offers by post from our trusted partners: companies operating in the clothing, collectables, food & wine, gardening, gadgets & entertainment, health & beauty, household goods, and home interiors categories. If you would like to receive these by post, please tick this box. ☐**

We respect your privacy. We use personal information you provide us with to send you information about our products, maintain records and for marketing purposes. For more information explaining how we use your information please see our privacy policy at www.pen-and-sword.co.uk/privacy. You can opt out of our mailing list at any time via our website or by calling 01226 734222.

Mr/Mrs/Ms ..............................................................................................................

Address.........................................................................................................................

Postcode................................ Email address.....................................................

**Website: www.pen-and-sword.co.uk  Email: enquiries@pen-and-sword.co.uk**
**Telephone: 01226 734555   Fax: 01226 734438**
**Stay in touch: facebook.com/penandswordbooks or follow us on Twitter @penswordbooks**

## Units of measurement

So far I have dealt with the definitions of various administrative units in Ireland across time, but another important consideration that needs to be understood in land research is the units of measurement that were created to physically reckon their size and shape, i.e. to help define their extent, as well as their value.

For example, in many records denoting land holdings you will often see area defined in acres, roods and perches, often abbreviated to A, R and P; a land holding at 4A 2R 27P means 4 acres, 2 roods and 27 perches. Whilst today we may think of an acre as a set area of land, in the past it often varied in size across the country.

An acre was originally the amount of land that a team of oxen could plough in a day, with the word acre originally deriving from the old Anglo-Saxon word *aecer*, meaning 'a field'. For most of the research we do between the early seventeenth-century Plantation period and 1824, the records we will look at usually involve what was known as the 'Irish acre' or 'plantation acre', measuring 7,840 square yards. This was based on the size of an acre commonly found in various parts of England, and adopted in Ireland during the Plantations. The plantation acre could be subdivided into 4 roods consisting of 40 perches each, with a perch being 7 square yards in size.

In 1824, not long after Ireland joined the United Kingdom, the system was changed to a series of smaller 'statute acres', with one plantation acre being the equivalent of 1.62 statute acres, or one statute acre being 4,840 square yards. This is important to note, because in records such as Griffith's Valuation (p.91), the measurement used is the statute acre, whereas in earlier records, such as tithe records (p.86), the system commonly used is the plantation acre. A conversion may be therefore necessary between different record sets when comparing them.

In terms of length measurements, the unit called a perch was 7 yards in length. Four perches made a chain and 40 perches a furlong, with 8 furlongs to the 'Irish mile' (meaning there were 32 chains, 320 perches or 2,240 yards to the Irish mile). Again, standardisation took place in 1824, with an Irish mile becoming the equivalent of 1.27 statute miles.

On currency, from 1701, thirteen Irish pounds were the equivalent of twelve English pounds, a situation which continued until 1826, at which point the Irish pound was formally abolished and sterling adopted. As with the English pound, there were 12 pence to the shilling, and 20 shillings to the pound, meaning that there were some 240 pence in the Irish pound.

Following its secession from the UK in 1922, the Free State continued to use sterling until 1928, until a new Irish pound (the punt) was once again introduced, pegged to the sterling rate on an equal pound to pound basis.

From the late 1960s, as with the UK, decimalisation was introduced in the Republic of Ireland, with one pound now containing 100 pence. After 1979, sterling and the punt diverged in value, and from 1999, the Republic of Ireland adopted the Euro as its currency, which it continues to use to this day. In the north, sterling has continued in use after Partition, and remains the currency in use there.

*Chapter 4*

# WHERE WERE THEY?

Many historic records can help us to build up the genealogical connections between relatives, within different family groups. In many cases, however, it is not only the names of people that will be mentioned, but also details of where they lived and when.

Arranging such records in a chronological order for our families can often tell us more about the family story. How long did a particular family stay at a residence? Did they reside in the same house for several generations, or regularly move between different addresses every few months, as those within sought new work opportunities?

With records such as censuses we can even find out some specific information about the nature of those properties, whether our ancestors owned their homes or were tenants to a landlord, and what quality of home they had. In some circumstances, we can even identify which outbuildings might have existed for their properties. With other census substitutes, such as street directories and electoral registers, we can identify clues to fill in the gaps to act as substitutes for the years for which the censuses themselves have sadly no longer survived.

## Vital records
The statutory civil registration of births, marriages and deaths commenced in Ireland in two phases. The registration of non-Roman Catholic marriages commenced in April 1845, whilst registration for all births, marriages and deaths, irrespective of religious denomination, began in January 1864. Although it was compulsory to register such events, there are gaps within the earlier records, in particular in those documenting births. The following geographical information is provided within each record type:

Birth records
- Place of birth for the child
- Dwelling place of the father
- The residence of the informant
- Registrar's District, Superintendent Registrar's District, and Poor Law Union

Marriage records
- Residence of each spouse at the time of marriage
- The name of the parish, county, denomination and church, or the registration office if a civil ceremony
- Registrar's District

Death records
- Place of death
- Residence of the informant
- Registrar's District, Superintendent Registrar's District, and Poor Law Union

There are some issues to be aware of with these documents:

- When they were recorded, it has often been the case in rural Ireland, historically, that the address given is simply that of the townland and civil parish, whereas in urban districts a more specific street address and house number may have been given.
- It is entirely possible that streets may have been renumbered across time – the number of your ancestor's house may have changed, and he or she may have never moved.
- With marriages it is also worth bearing in mind that the addresses or residences given were those at the time of the wedding, and may not necessarily have been permanent addresses of residence.
- The recorded place of death may itself deceive, and not necessarily be the usual place where the deceased actually lived usually, it may well have been somewhere where he or she simply received their final days of care. On many records within my family, for example, the address of death is listed as 51 Lisburn Road in Belfast – this is not a home address, but that of the Belfast Union Workhouse, which had its own infirmary (and which is now the address of the modern Belfast City Hospital).

As noted in Chapter 3, events were registered locally in Registrars' Districts/Dispensary Districts, with copies of registers conveyed to the

Superintendent Registrar, and then onwards to the General Register Office in Dublin. Records for these events for the whole of Ireland up to 1921 are freely available at **www.irishgenealogy.ie**, and then for the Republic only after this. For privacy reasons, the site respects closure periods for births for the most recent hundred years, marriages for the most recent seventy-five years, and deaths for the most recent fifty years. When searching for events on this site you will need to know the name of the relevant Superintendent Registrar's District to localise your searches. More recent records for the Republic can be obtained via **www.gov.ie/gro** (or via **www.certificates.ie**), and at the GRO's research facility in Werburgh Street, Dublin (see the GRO site for details).

*The Irish government's Irish Genealogy records platform.*

In Northern Ireland, historic records from 1845 onwards have been digitised and made available online via the pay per view General Register Office for Northern Ireland (GRONI) site at **https://geni.nidirect.gov.uk**, with similar closure periods in place. Searches can be carried out using the Superintendent Registrar's District, and narrowed further to the local Registrar's District. More recent records must be obtained as expensive certified extracts from GRONI in Belfast via **www.nidirect.gov.uk/general-register-office-for-northern-ireland**, although these can be consulted in digital form also on terminals at the GRONI facility itself, and on a small number of terminals at the Public Record Office of Northern Ireland (PRONI).

Prior to civil registration, the records to turn to are those of the parish churches. Whilst some registers in more urban areas may record street addresses, residential information within church registers can be often quite sparse, however, and in many cases will often note the townland of occupation only – if even that. James G. Ryan's *Irish Church Records, New Edition* (Flyleaf Press, 2001) provides a comprehensive overview of the registers kept by the Quakers, Church of Ireland, Presbyterian churches, Roman Catholic churches, Methodists, Jews, Huguenots and Baptists. Note that with Roman Catholic records the parishes named in such records may differ to the civil parishes in which they were registered. For further information on the various different Presbyterian church denominations, consult William J. Roulston's *Researching Presbyterian Ancestors in Ireland* (Ulster Historical Foundation, 2020).

Most online data providers concentrate on providing the information for baptisms, marriages and deaths/burials, but the churches did generate many other significant records detailing parish business, such as the Church of Ireland's vestry records, and the Presbyterian kirk

*Whitechurch civil parish, Co. Kilkenny. Amongst the responsibilities of the general vestry was the maintenance of parish infrastructure, including the building and repair of minor roads.*

session registers. These are equally as important to consult, if they have survived, as they may carry information about areas within the parish, as well as additional location information for individuals discussed.

The Church of Ireland was the state church up to 1871, and as such, the Anglican vestry minutes and burial registers prior to this may well note people from other denominations, for a variety of issues. These may include the election of wardens (two per parish, and not necessarily members of the Anglican Church), those paying the 'parish cess' (p.66), members appointed to repair the road network, parishioners in receipt of poor relief or who were licensed to beg, seat holders in the parish church, those confirmed as members, and in some cases, even information about vital events such as baptisms, marriages and deaths/burials.

A guide to help locate surviving vestry records at the Representative Church Body Library in Dublin is available at **www.ireland.anglican. org/about/rcb-library/online-parish-records**, whilst the *PRONI Guide to Church Records* can also advise on material available at PRONI in Belfast at **www.nidirect.gov.uk/publications/proni-guide-church-records**.

## The 1813 census

Following the passage of the Census (Ireland) Act 1812, the first nationwide census of Ireland within the UK was commenced in 1813, but was so poorly administered by the Grand Juries of the counties involved, who had been entrusted with the task, that its findings were never presented to the British parliament.

An interesting article on the reasons for the census' failure is available on the University of Essex's Online Historical Population Reports website, better known as 'Histpop', at **https://tinyurl.com/1813census**.

## Decennial census records (1821–51)

Realising what a disaster the 1813 exercise had been, a new Act was passed in 1815 to entrust the recording of the census in 1821 to local magistrates at Quarter Sessions and assistant barristers, who then appointed local enumerators to the task. There was no single 'census night' for this or the following 1831 census, with the exercise taking several weeks. In 1841, members of the Royal Irish Constabulary were appointed to the task as enumerators, and the census was then recorded on a single day, a pattern followed in subsequent exercises.

Tragically, only some census fragments exist for parts of the country from 1821–51, with the surviving fragments now digitised and made available at **www.genealogy.nationalarchives.ie** and **www.census. nationalarchives.ie**.

Of the records that have survived, some are the original returns, whilst others are surviving copies of information extracted from the originals, for which the originals no longer exist. With the notable exceptions of surviving 1831 census details for County Londonderry and for 1851 in Dublin, which both list heads of households only, most will name members present in each household on the designated census night, along with additional information such as their ages and occupations.

Although the online databases favour searching by name, it is again advisable to browse through the returns for any given area, as further information might be provided which is not indexed. Browsing the records for the townland of Rathreddy in the parish of Kilconickny in County Galway, for example, reveals a note written by the enumerator in the 'Observations' column of the second page about the difficulties of establishing the boundaries for the area to be recorded, as well as some useful information about the townland itself:

> On this townland stands the ruins of the Old Castle of Rathreddy, or Raruddy.
>
> Also a Burial Ground for Children.
>
> The remainder of the Townland of Rathreddy is in the Barony of Loughrea in this Parish.
>
> As it is impossible to ascertain the means & bounds Between the Baronies of Athenry and Loughrea on this Townland I have taken an Acc[oun]t. of the inhabitants of [the] Whole Townland which from the situation of the house (they being principally adjoining that part of the Barony of Athenry which next meets this Townland) I concluded the entire, or at least, the principal part are situate in the Barony of Athenry.
>
> From the impossibility to ascertain the Bounds the Landholders are alleged to pay half their Public & Grand Jury Cess in each barony.
>
> Edw. Doyle., Enr.

The earlier censuses do not contain the same detailed returns on the property owned, but the observations recorded for individuals may include additional information about the person being enumerated. In the same 1821 County Galway census, for example, an entry for 50-year-old farmer and smith, Thomas Huban, in the townland of Clashagany in Kiltullagh parish also notes that he 'holds 9 acres in the Townlands of Carrakeel in this parish'. Such detail pre-dates even the tithe applotment records (p.86) for the area.

## Census extracts for Old Age Pension applications

Some additional material from the 1841 and 1851 censuses was copied prior to the destruction of the original registers, to support claims for the Old Age Pension, as introduced by the UK government from 1909. There were several forms generated as part of the application process, which required claimants to prove that they were at least 70 years old. This was difficult for many people, in that civil registration of births had only commenced in Ireland in 1864, meaning that alternative sources were required in the form of extracts from either parish records or census returns from 1841 and 1851.

Historic applications to the Public Record Office in Dublin for census verifications have now been digitised by the National Archives of Ireland and made available online at **www.genealogy.nationalarchives.ie** and **http://censussearchforms.nationalarchives.ie**. The records are freely available, and can be searched by the applicant's name, the names of his or her parents, the census year searched, and by residency details, with claimants noted from across Ireland. Many of these applications were unsuccessful, but for those who were found in the censuses, the details for the whole family were extracted.

Take for example an application made by Bridget Kearns in 1917, who gave her address at that point as being that of a Mr. J. Hoye, R.I.C., Mullingar. To request a pension, Bridget sought an extract from the 1851 census for the County Sligo-based townland of Mullanabreena, within the civil parish of Achonry, and barony of Leyny. In her claim, she advised that her parents' names were Hugh and Hanna Kearns, maiden name Healy. The request was received by the PRO on 21 September 1917, with a search duly carried out within the census books just four days later on 25 September. Bridget and her parents were duly found, with the record noting Hugh and Hanna 'Kerins' to have married in 1831, and Bridget herself noted as being aged 12 in the census. A formal extract from the record was made on 1 October and despatched to the applicant just two days later.

Along with the ability to search for an individual, I can of course also search by geographic terms. If I was to search for others who claimed to have lived in the townland of Mullanabreena, for example, I find two other pension claimants who requested extracts from the 1851 census, a Catherine Snee (based in Scotland) and a Catherine Golden (in Ballymote, Co. Sligo), who may well have been known to Bridget's family.

Many applications from overseas claimants are also included in the record set. Utilising the 'Applicant's present address' search field, returns are presented for the following named countries as examples:

- Scotland 387
- England 263
- Wales 40
- Australia 87
- New Zealand 46 (27 of them for the New Zealand High Commission in London)
- Canada 8
- South Africa 5
- USA 32

Further returns can be found when searching with more specific or varied terms. For example, a search for Glasgow returns some 603 applications, Edinburgh 626, Dundee 47, London 410, Birmingham 43, Manchester 219, Bristol 13, Cardiff 18, and Swansea 5. On a similar basis, using state names in the USA provides a further 50 returns for New York, 15 for New Jersey, and 7 for Massachusetts. Abbreviations provide further returns, with 'Mass' offering a further 37 entries for Massachusetts.

Copies of an additional document in the application process, known as a `Form 37', are also held at PRONI in Belfast for the north. Whilst there is an index of sorts available at the facility on microfilm, the information returned does not in fact quite connect up with the way that the returns are presented in their bound volumes. A key detail not given in the index is the barony in which the applications have been collated, a detail you will certainly need in order to try to find an entry of interest within the large bound volumes. I was fortunate to discover a record within these volumes for my three times great-grandfather Arthur Taylor in the townland of Belfast, in the civil parish of Shankill, and barony of Upper Belfast, with the original record turning out to be something of a goldmine with what was revealed – despite the fact that he was never actually found in the records.

Arthur Taylor was born in Belfast in 1848 and made an application for a pension in 1918. To do so he required proof of age, and so asked for a search of the 1851 census, stating in his application that he had lived as a child at Abbey Street near Peter's Hill with his parents Arthur Taylor and Isabella Hall. The search was duly carried out by the pension authorities, but he could not be located at that address. Undeterred, he asked for another search, stating that as a child he had also lived for a time with his grandfather, named as Arthur Taylor, at a place that was either called McLelland's Lane, McLelland's Entry, or possibly Lime Street – as a child at the time his memory had obviously been quite vague. Again the authorities carried out a search, and discovered that there was indeed an Arthur Taylor there with his wife Ann, noting that they had married in 1819 (as recorded in the census) – but once again there was no sign of Arthur Taylor, the applicant. Still undaunted, Arthur made a third attempt, suggesting that he had also lived as a child at both Cargill Street and Cargill Court. Once again the authorities found no trace of him.

On the negative side, the fact that Arthur could not be found in the 1851 census was a blow, in that the details of his immediate family could not be located. On the plus side, however, the very process of trying to find him led to me discovering several addresses where he claimed to have lived as a child in the late 1840s and early 1850s, as well as the names of his grandparents, the year in which they had married, and the part of Belfast in which they had resided.

## Decennial census records (1861–1891)

Virtually nothing from the 1861–1891 censuses has survived, although there are limited exceptions with some information extracted by Catholic priests and included within parish registers. None of these are available at **www.genealogy.nationalarchives.ie**.

Some information extracted from the 1861 census for the Catholic parish of Enniscorthy in County Wexford is presented on the Catholic Parish Registers at the NLI website at **https://registers.nli.ie**, within microfilm 04250/02. The records are headed 'Census of the Inhabitants of the Parish of Enniscorthy commenced April 17th 1861' and list the number of a house, inhabitants, and whether Catholic or Protestant (or a total number given of the number of Catholics or Protestants found within). The information is very basic, with mainly names noted, but some occasional extra details are occasionally offered, with individuals noted as 'Senior', for example, or their marital status if widowed.

Transcribed information from the 1871 census return for the Catholic parish of Drumconrath in County Meath is also available on the site, under microfilm 04184/05. Headed 'Registry of all person who slept in the following thirty-three townlands on the night of Sunday, 2 April 1871, Also the names of some who were only temporarily absent', the document is presented in order of townland, with the individual entries listing the names of those enumerated, their ages and sex, relationship to the head of household (including marital status, and whether illegitimate, if known), and a remarks column, which essentially notes any comments on religious adherence for non-Catholics.

A transcribed version of the information is also freely available on the Irish Genealogical Research Society's website as a PDF document, recorded as the 'Drumcondra/Loughbrackan 1871 Census Fragment', at

**www.irishancestors.ie/resources/unique-resources/drumcondra-loughbrackan-1871-census-fragment**.

## Decennial census records (1901–1911)

The only complete censuses to have survived from the pre-Partition period are those for 1901 and 1911. These have been digitised and made freely available online at **www.genealogy.nationalarchives.ie** and **www.census.nationalarchives.ie**. Although very little has survived from the earlier returns, some fragments have (which will be discussed shortly), whilst the printed returns from information collated from the various censuses is available, which can help to determine changes in an area's population in an area over time.

One of the great advantages with the 1901 and 1911 censuses is that the original household schedules have survived. In addition to naming individuals present on census night, these original documents, filled in by the head of household (or by the enumerator if the head was illiterate), carry an incredible amount of information on the land holding itself. Several forms were included, which will be found as digitised images within the 'View Census Images' box on the search results page. For most households these documents will normally include a Household Return (Form A), an Enumerator's Abstract (Form N), a House and Building Return (Form B1), and an Out-Offices and Farm-Steadings (Form B2).

Although the address is not recorded on the front of Form A, it is to be found located on the rear of the document – if digitised, that is

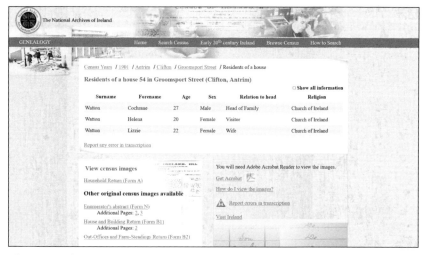

*The 1901 and 1911 census search page offers access to the original householder return, Form A, but also additional images, including Form N, Form B1 and Form B2.*

– which is not always the case on the online presentation, particularly for the 1901 census. If it has been scanned, a link will be found by the 'Additional pages' tag under the main Form A household schedule page link. The geographic boundaries that can be identified from this part of the main schedule form were the County, Poor Law Union, District Electoral Division, Barony, Parish, Townland, City, Borough, Division, Urban District, Town or Village, and lastly, Street &c with No. of House. The last box contains the name of the head of household.

If we take, for example, the 1911 census for my three times great-grandfather John Holmes, who resided in Raphoe, County Donegal, we find that he is listed in a Form A schedule as being in a household of just one person, i.e. himself. He is recorded as John Holmes, Head of Family, Presbyterian, able to read and write, 73 years of age, a retired bootmaker, a widower, and born in County Donegal. On the reverse of this page, the address details are given as follows:

| | |
|---|---|
| County | Donegal |
| Poor Law Union | Strabane |
| District Electoral Division | Raphoe |
| Barony | Raphoe North |
| Parish | Raphoe |
| Townland | Raphoe Town Parks |
| City | ------ |
| Parliamentary Borough | ------ |
| Parliamentary Division | East Donegal |
| Urban District | ------ |
| Town or Village | ------ |
| Street &c with No. of House | ------ |

Whilst the front page of Form A includes the details of those who were in the household, another often overlooked detail to be aware of is that found in the top right of this page, where there is a section that states 'No. on Form B'. In the above example, the 'No. on Form B' for John's entry is noted as being '11'. This number equates to the line number on the separate Forms N and B1 accompanying his household schedule, which include further substantial details about the property itself, as will be noted shortly.

Much of the address information given in Form A is usually repeated at the top of Form N, the enumerator's abstract page, alongside a signed declaration by the enumerator. This page primarily returns statistical information drawn from the household schedules, with each line corresponding to the line number which matches the 'No. on Form B' mentioned on Form A. As well as noting how many males and females there were in each property, the page also notes how many dwelling houses there were on a plot of land, and whether they were 'inhabited', 'uninhabited' or 'building' (i.e. under construction).

Form B1 is considerably more useful for property-based research. As with Form N, the administrative boundaries are repeated at the top of the page, and once again, using the 'No. on Form B' previously found on Form A as a line number for the relevant household, we can identify some useful information about the nature of the property itself, thanks to a series of detailed questions. There are two broad categories requiring responses, 'Houses' and 'Families &c'. Under 'Houses', some general introductory details kick things off:

Column 1    No. of House or Building
Column 2    Whether Built or Building
Column 3    State Whether Private Dwelling, Public Building, School, Manufactory, Hotel, Public-house, Lodging-house, or Shop, &c.
Column 4    Number of Out-Offices and Farm-steadings as returned on Form B2
Column 5    Is House inhabited? – Yes or No, as the case may be

There then follows a more forensic examination of the nature of the house, with questions answered according to a formula to determine what 'class' of house was there:

## PARTICULARS OF INHABITED HOUSES

Column 6: WALLS
    If Walls are of Stone, Brick, or Concrete, enter the figure 1 in this column: if they are of Mud, Wood, or other perishable material, enter the figure 0

Column 7: ROOF
    If Roof is of Slate, iron, or Tiles, enter the figure 1 in this column: if it is of Thatch, Wood, or other perishable material, enter the figure 0

Column 8: ROOMS
    Enter in this column:-
    For each House with

| | |
|---|---|
| 1 Room only, the figure | 1 |
| For Houses with | |
| 2, 3 or 4 room | 2 |
| 5 or 6 | 3 |
| 7, 8, or 9 | 4 |
| 10, 11, or 12 | 5 |
| 13 or more | 6 |

Column 9: WINDOWS IN FRONT
State in this column the Exact number of Windows in Front of House

Column 10: Tot the Figures you have entered in columns 6, 7, 8 & 9 and enter the Total for each House in this column

Column 11: CLASS OF HOUSE
When Total in Col 1 is:
1 or 2, enter '4th'
3, 4 or 5, enter '3rd'
6, 7, 8, 9, 10, or 11, enter '2nd'
12 or over, enter '1st'

The 'Families &c' section has various further questions concerning the occupants, some of which further add to the information about the house itself:
Column 12: No. of distinct Families in each House

Column 13: Name of the Head of the Family residing in the House

Column 14: No. of rooms occupied by each family

Column 15: Total number of persons in each family

Column 16: Date on which Form A was collected

Column 17: Number of Person who were sick on 31st March, 1901

---

* There is in fact a further sub-note appended for the Column 14 instruction, at the foot of the page: 'If one Room is occupied by more than one Family, the Names of the Heads of the Families so occupying it should be bracketed together… and the figure entered in Col. 14 opposite the middle of the bracket.'

Column 18: Names of Landholder (if any) on whose Holding the House is situated, whether that name appears in Col.13 or not

Column 19: No. on Form M1 if House is on the Holding of a Land Holder

Notice that Column 13 asks for the 'Name of Head of the Family residing in the House'. This does not mean the head of the property as a whole, but of a family unit, and it is often the case that more than one family may have lived within the same building. As such, you might well find that several household schedules exist for the same property which may not be immediately apparent from Form A itself. Again, the clue to unlock if this is the case is the 'No. on Form B1' on the Form A schedule.

If we return to the 1911 census for my Raphoe-based three times great-grandfather John Holmes, his Form A entry lists only himself as present in the household. The 'No. on Form B' is given as 11, and when we look at the relevant Form B1, there is only one line of information, which notes that John lived in a third-class house with a single room, and only one window within that room. His landlord was noted as James McCobb.

So far, so good. However, if we now go back ten years to the earlier 1901 census, John's circumstances were slightly different. As with 1911, the 1901 return shows a Form A listing only John as the occupant in his household. The form at this stage notes that he was aged 60, and once again, a widower. In the top right corner of this particular form its states that the No. on Form B is 4.

If we now take a look at Form B1, and look down to line 4, far from finding a single line of information, we in fact find two. The first line concerns John, but on the subsequent line there is further information about another head of household, Martha Allison.

The statistical information on the property helps to clarify the situation. Asked how many distinct families there were in each house, the number '2' is given. John is noted as occupying one room, and as being in a family of one. Martha is similarly described. Their landlord is again given as 'James McCobb of Raphoe Town'. The house is also stated to have two rooms, with John occupying the front room, which had two windows. If we now do another search to find Martha Allison in Raphoe, she turns up in a completely separate Form A household schedule, again listing only herself as resident, in which she is described as an 81-year-old widow from County Tyrone.

Piecing all of this together, we can now see that John and Martha, unrelated, were both tenants in the same property in Raphoe Town Parks in 1901, paying rent to James McCobb, and with each of them occupying a single room. Ten years later, John had moved to a much smaller property, with only one room and a single window, but still noted as a tenant of the same landlord. As a development in John's story, none of this is revealed by using the Form A documents alone from each census.

Although the landlord's name is given on Form B, you unfortunately cannot directly search for a landlord's full portfolio of properties, you can only do a keyword search for him or her as the head of a household. What you can do, however, is to browse through the book for the relevant townland or townlands where you may think that your ancestor owned property. On the 1901 Form B return for John Holmes, James McCobb of Raphoe Town Parks was not just noted as the landlord for John's house, he in fact had six properties and seven tenants, and may well have had more, identified on other pages.

You can browse as many records as you like via the search page at **http://www.census.nationalarchives.ie/search/**, by utilising the section to the right of the 'Search' area marked 'Browse'. Clicking on the 'Browse by place' link within this allows you to access a list of counties; further clicking on one of these brings up a list of DEDs for that county, and clicking on the name of a DED then returns a list of all the townlands or streets within it.

In the above example for John Holmes, clicking on 'Raphoe' as the name of the DED in Donegal provides the following additional townland options that can be browsed within:

- Beltany
- Bogagh
- Cooladerry
- Coolaghy Glebe
- Cottown
- Drumineney
- Gortaquigley
- Guest End Street
- Irish Street
- Lismontigley
- Lisnoble
- Magheraboy
- Magherahaan
- Main Street
- McBride Street
- Meeting House Street
- Milltown
- Oakfield Demesne
- Raphoe Demesne
- Raphoe Townparks (where John was found)
- Shannagh
- Sheep Lane
- Stranorlaghan
- The Close
- Tops
- Tops Demesne
- William Street

It may well be that James McCobb had additional properties for which he was the landlord, which can be identified by examining these local townland areas. An alternative way to try to find such information may be to examine the Valuation Revision Books, aka Cancelled Land Books, for the period and areas in question, either at the Valuation Office in Dublin (p.9) or through the online holdings available for Northern Ireland via the PRONI website (p.4).

The final part of the 1901 and 1911 censuses is Form B2, the Out-Offices and Farm-Steadings Return. The instruction for the enumerator was noted at the top of the page:

> The Enumerator will return on this Form all Out-offices intended for Domestic or Agricultural purposes, but he should not include any Out-offices intended for Sanitary Accommodation, such as Privies, Ashpits, &c.; or for Horticultural Purposes, such as Conservatories, Green-houses, &c.; or for Pleasure, such as Summer-houses Tea-houses, &c.

Beneath this is a list of the 'No. of Form B' numbers on the left side in a vertical column, alongside which the enumerator was to tick whether any of the following were present:

- Stable
- Coach House
- Harness Room
- Cow House
- Calf House
- Dairy
- Piggery
- Fowl House
- Boiling House
- Barn
- Turf House
- Potato House
- Workshop
- Shed
- Store
- Forge
- Laundry

A final section allowed for 'Other Out-offices' to be recorded, up to a maximum of five.

## Subsequent censuses

Due to the Troubles of the early 1920s, the 1921 census was postponed, and it would not be until 1926 that the next census was carried out. By now the island of Ireland had been partitioned, but despite this division, the census was carried out on 18–19 April 1926 in both territories. The records for Northern Ireland have sadly not survived, but those for the Free State will be released in a few years' time.

From this point onwards the frequency of census gathering, both in Northern Ireland and in the Free State (later the Republic), became irregular. Following 1926, censuses for Northern Ireland were carried out in 1937, 1951, 1961, 1966, 1971, and every tenth year thereafter, up to 2021. All the records have survived, but are closed to public access for 100 years for privacy reasons. The census in 1937 was a more limited exercise, omitting questions on occupation and industry, and although a 1941 census was intended, it was aborted as a consequence of the Second World War. The surviving 1939 National Identity Register makes for a partial substitute (p.62).

In addition to the 2021 census being carried out in Northern Ireland during the coronavirus pandemic, an informal voluntary-based 'Stay Home Census' was also carried out by PRONI (**www.nidirect.gov. uk/publications/stay-home-census**), seeking information for future generations on how people responded to the pandemic during the 'lockdown' periods of high infection. These are catalogued under D447, but are closed to public access. The questions asked included:

Address (town only):
Date:
Name:
Surname:
Relation to Person 1:
Age (at last Birthday):
Gender:
Place of Birth (town, county or country):
Did you lockdown in your usual residence?
Occupation (or current education level):
Work status during lockdown (i.e. keyworker, WFH, furlough):
Describe the lockdown in one word:

In the south, following 1926, the census was taken much more frequently, with further enumerations in 1936, 1946, 1951, 1956, 1961, 1966, 1971, 1979, 1981, 1986, 1991, 1996, 2002, 2006, 2011 and 2016.

The Irish census planned for 2021 was postponed until April 2022 as a consequence of the coronavirus pandemic.

## Census reports
Although the original householder schedules and enumerators copies from many of the censuses have not survived, it is possible to view the information collated afterwards through the many census reports published by the respective governments involved.

Census reports from 1821 to 1911 are available on the Online Historical Population Reports Project at **www.histpop.org** (or **www2.histpop.org**).

Census reports for the Republic of Ireland from 1926 to 2006 are available from the Central Statistics Office (*An Phríomh-Oifig Saidrimh*) at **www.cso.ie/en/census/censusreports1821-2006**.

Northern Ireland reports from 1926 to 2011 are available through the Northern Ireland Statistics and Research Agency at **www.nisra.gov.uk/statistics/census**.

## 1939 National Identity Register (Northern Ireland)

No regular census was carried out in the UK in 1941, because of the Second World War, but on 29 September 1939 an emergency census was carried out by the British government for the purposes of issuing identity cards and a possible personnel draft. As a continuing member of the UK, Northern Ireland was included within this vast exercise, and its records have survived and are held at PRONI. They are accessible to view because no formal closure period has been imposed upon them (as with the decennial censuses), for they were never officially categorised as a census when the legislation was passed for their creation.

The Northern Irish returns are the only records within the UK for which you do not yet have to pay a fee. To access them you need to make a Freedom of Information (FOI) request to PRONI, through the archive's enquiry service.

A useful example of what to expect from these records comes from an application I made for information on my grandfather Charles Paton at his house in the Greencastle area of Belfast. To facilitate the request, I had to supply the address at which he was resident in 1939 and to provide a scanned copy of his death certificate. Information is only provided for those enumerated who are now deceased, for whom data protection laws no longer apply.

The details contained were limited, but in my case were extremely useful. I received my grandfather's name, his occupation and date of birth. He was listed as a branch manager at this point, confirming why he had moved from Scotland to Belfast just three years before (same firm), but crucially he was also described as having been born in 1905. Although Charles Paton eventually died in Donaghadee in 1989, he had actually been born in Belgium to Scottish parents, but the information I had previously sourced on his birth (from other sources) was both vague and conflicting. This date, however, was given by Charles himself – and on the basis of this record I was finally able to locate a baptismal record for him in Belgium.

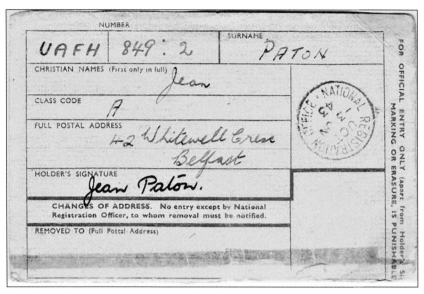

*Identity card issued to the author's grandmother Jean Paton in the Second World War.*

## Earlier censuses

There were many other censuses carried out prior to the decennial censuses from 1821, some as enumerations of the population for civic purposes, and others for religious reasons.

Whilst not all are as detailed as the modern post-1821 censuses, there were exceptions. The 116-page-long 1799 Carrick-on-Suir census in County Tipperary, for example, which is held at the British Library (but with copies at the National Library of Ireland and at Waterford Library), listed everyone in the household along with ages, marital status and occupations. Compiled by Francis White, William Morton Pitt (a cousin of the British Prime Minster) and Patrick Lynch, it was a truly massive undertaking carried out when the town was under martial law, following the United Irishmen uprising a year earlier. The census enumerated 10,907 people in 1,738 houses within both Carrick Mor, County Tipperary, and Carrick Beg, County Waterford, which face each other on either side of the River Suir.

A brief snapshot of twenty complete households from this census has been transcribed and preserved at **https://web.archive.org/web/20150906202304/http://www.igp-web.com/tipperary/1799_carrick.htm**, which provides an idea of how detailed the returns were. The Irish Genealogical Research Society also offers a members-only database of the full census at **www.irishancestors.ie/search/carrick_on_suir/index.php**,

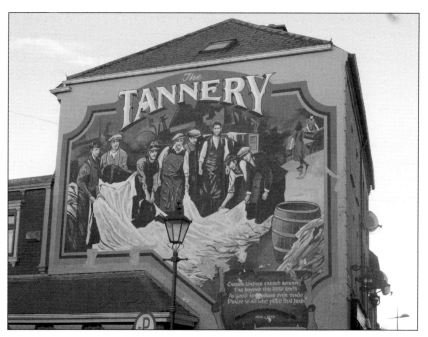

*Mural in Carrick-on-Suir commemorating the town's tanning trade.*

although a free basic search is provided. In 1987, the Royal Irish Academy published *The Demography of Carrick-on-Suir, 1799*, by L. A. Clarkson (Proceedings, Volume 87, C, Number 2), which analysed its many findings.

At the other extreme, some censuses were, frustratingly, recorded purely for statistical purposes, such as an exercise carried out by Arthur Thomson in Belfast in 1807. This returned the information that the city comprised some 22,095 people at that stage, living in 3,514 houses. There were 7,213 males aged 10 years and upwards, and 9,227 females, as well as 3,011 males under 10 years of age, and 2,644 females. Sadly none of the names appear to have been recorded, or to have survived if they were.

The 1803 Agricultural Census was carried out during the Napoleonic period, for which returns exist for parts of Counties Antrim and Down. The records are held at the NAI and PRONI, with many names available through online transcriptions. Following the Famine, agricultural censuses were then carried out on every farm in Ireland annually from 1847 up to Partition, and in its aftermath in both the north and south. The Central Statistics Office's Farming Since the Famine 1847-1996 site at **www.cso.ie/ en/statistics/othercsopublications/farmingsincethefamine1847-1996/** carries the statistical information generated, and a useful history on Irish agriculture in this period; the equivalent for the north is to be found at **www.daera-ni.gov.uk/articles/agricultural-census-historical-data**.

The 1796 Flax Growers List, which lists those in receipt of spinning wheels and looms from the Irish Linen Board to help promote the linen industry, has been transcribed at **https://failteromhat.com/flax1796.php**.

Pender's Census of 1659 covers all of Ireland, with the exception of Cavan, Galway, Mayo, Tyrone and Wicklow. Four baronies are also missing for County Cork and nine from Meath. This census was compiled by Sir William Petty (p.83), and later published in 1939 by Seamus Pender of the Irish Manuscripts Commission, hence the given name. This printed edition, *A Census of Ireland Circa 1659, With Supplementary Material from the Poll Money Ordinances (1600–1661)*, can be accessed online through the website of the Irish Manuscripts Commission (p.11).

The Ulster Historical Foundation has published *Men and Arms: The Ulster Settlers, c. 1630*, an equally useful list, drawn up to find out how many weapons the recently planted settlers could muster in the event of an uprising. It effectively acts as a census substitute, detailing some 8,000 families in the province, with their names arranged by county and barony. Edited by R. J. Hunter, it includes annotations from years of research into other sources such as the 1641 Depositions (p.21), which make it easy for many of the names to be identified.

Later in the same decade, the Great Parchment Book for Derry is another useful resource detailing those who worked for the livery companies that had invested in the development of Londonderry (p.X). It has been digitised and made available at **www.greatparchmentbook.org**.

Another early surviving enumeration is the Census of the Fews from 1602, drawn up under the authority of Turlagh MacHenry O'Neill, concerning a barony in County Armagh for which he was chief. A transcript is available at **https://web.archive.org/web/20200130082529/http://www.mcconville.org/main/genealogy/census1602.html**.

## Early taxation
Various forms of taxation were also levied in Ireland which can assist, some of which related to property qualifications.

Poll tax – this tax was levied in the 1660s, with surviving poll book returns arranged by townland, and noting the taxpayer, occupation, and amount due.

Subsidies – these were payments made in the 1630s and 1660s by the wealthier in society as a grant to the Crown. Various subsidy rolls are held at the NAI, the NLI and at PRONI.

<u>Hearth money</u> – a hearth tax was levied twice a year in Ireland from 1662 until 1800, initially at a rate of 2s per hearth for every householder. From 1793, those with one hearth and personal property valued at less than £10, or with a house and land below the value of £5, became exempt from the tax, whilst from 1795 all of those with a single hearth became exempt. The tax was abandoned completely following the Act of Union, it having disappeared in England over a century before in 1689. The original records were destroyed in 1922, but many copies have survived, which can be accessed at the NAI and PRONI.

The locations of the surviving records for all of these taxation lists, and others, are noted in John Grenham's *Tracing Your Irish Ancestors*, which provides a valuable county by county guide for the whole island, with a similar offering within William J. Roulston's *Researching Ulster Ancestors* for the nine counties of Ulster. Details for both books are noted on p.149. Many of the records have also been published, with their titles accessible from the NLI catalogue at **http://catalogue.nli.ie**.

Also payable within parishes was the 'parish cess' or 'vestry assessment', which was used for various parochial functions such as poor relief, and which was not abolished until 1833 by the Church Temporalities (Ireland) Act. Payments from these may be noted within the various surviving vestry minutes for Anglican parishes (p.49).

In many larger towns with majority Catholic populations, including Dublin, Cork, Waterford and Limerick, the 'minister's money' was another tax charged from 1665 to 1857, with the money raised by churchwardens four times a year on the quarter days, for the support of the Church of Ireland minister, which caused much resentment.

## Ecclesiastical censuses
Various other census type exercises were carried out by churches to enumerate their congregations, whilst several religious censuses were also recorded across the country at various stages, which may equally be of assistance.

The National Archives of Ireland website has a thirty-three-page long document in PDF format at **www.nationalarchives.ie/PDF/ ReligiousCensus.pdf**, which lists the archival repositories across Ireland holding copies of material from the 1766 Religious Census of Ireland, carried out in March 1766 by order of the Irish House of Lords. The original census was destroyed in 1922, but transcripts exist for many parishes, as compiled by genealogist Tenison Groves prior to the Civil War. PRONI includes information from this census in its free-to-access 'Name Search' database at **www.nidirect.gov.uk/information-and- services/search-archives-online/name-search**.

The census contains entries from most of Ulster's counties, with the exception of Monaghan, and additional material for parishes in the counties of Cork Dublin, Kildare, Laois (Queen's County), Limerick, Longford, Louth, Meath, Offaly (King's County), Tipperary, Wexford, Westmeath and Wicklow.

PRONI's database also includes surviving data from the 1740s Protestant Householders Returns for counties Antrim, Armagh, Donegal, Down, Londonderry and Tyrone, and the 1775 Dissenters' Petitions list, noting Presbyterians who were discriminated against by the Penal Laws by the Irish Parliament in 1691 (p.22), by having the right to vote at Anglican vestry meetings removed. The 1775 petitions also include the names of some Anglican protesters, and the Parliament's Act was repealed a year later.

The different churches also recorded information about parishioners at a more local level. For example the Church of Ireland parish may have listed members within its vestry records, Presbyterian denominations within their kirk session papers, and Roman Catholic parish priests may have recorded members within their *status animarum* ('state of the souls') books.

A good example of a *status animarum* record which can be found online is that for a household from the Roman Catholic parish of Woodford (civil parish of Ballynakill) in County Galway in 1889. It notes the names

*County Galway, Ireland.*

of members of the Ward family as being in the 'district' (townland) of Loughatorick, with the father James a 32-year-old farmer, his 28-year-old wife 'Mrs Ward', their three children, and a lodger. As a church census, it further notes that the couple's daughter Mary Anne, aged 4, had received her first communion. This particular record is not identified on the NLI's Roman Catholic records platform at **https://registers.nli. ie**, but was instead found on FamilySearch at **www.familysearch.org/ ark:/61903/3:1:3Q9M-C9BB-Y9QT-4?i=1759**, when looking there for records for the Catholic parish of Woodford.

A very small number of additional Roman Catholic Church censuses have been transcribed on RootsIreland (**www.rootsireland.ie**), for example the Co. Galway West parishes of Kinvara (1834) and Spiddal (1884 and 1895), and for the Co. Limerick parishes of St. Patrick's (1830 and 1835), Pallasgrean (1834) and Athea (1857).

In the Presbyterian records, I was fortunate to locate information about my five times great-grandparents John Bill and Mary Gibb in a church census record from 1831 within the County Antrim-based congregation at Templepatrick. Described as 'A list of the families belonging to the Orthodox Congregation of Templepatrick in the first visitation in 1831 by the Rev J. Carr', it noted John and Mary as being resident in the townland of Ballycushin, and their children as being David, Elizabeth, John, William Wallace, and Daniel. In a subsequent census of 1857 for the church, 'A list of the families in connection with the Orthodox Congregation of Templepatrick – visitation commenced on the 3d of March 1857', John was not present, having already passed away, but his wife was noted as 'Widow M. Bill', accompanied by her children David, Margaret and Eliza Gray. (Both censuses were consulted at PRONI on microfilm MIC 1P/325A/1).

These records were particularly useful for my family research when combined with information found from the newspaper coverage of an extraordinary and tragic incident in 1871. The Eliza Gray noted in the 1857 record was the mother of a woman called Margaret Langtry, who on 30 October 1874 was murdered in Ballycushan townland at the house of her uncle David Bill. The alleged killer was her first cousin William Wallace Bill (son of John Bill, noted as a child to John and Mary in 1831), who was tried in Belfast in the following year and found not guilty. The detail found within the newspaper coverage, combined with the church censuses from 1831 and 1857, and other vital and land-based records, allowed me to very safely reconstitute the various family branches of the Bill family in the area back to the late eighteenth century.

There are many similar resources including unofficial censuses and muster rolls available from a variety of repositories around Ireland. Again, many are listed in John Grenham's and William J. Roulston's respective guides (p.149).

In addition, a series of county-based *Tracing Your [county] Ancestors* guides from Flyleaf Press (**www.flyleaf.ie**) contain further useful source lists for many counties in the Republic, whilst the *Researching Your Ancestors in the North of Ireland* county guides from the North of Ireland Family History Society (**www.nifhs.org/product-category/booklets-county**) carry similar listings for the province of Ulster.

Some further census listings and substitutes for Ireland are identified in the Federation of Family History Societies guide, *Local Census Listings 1522–1930: Holdings in the British Isles* (3rd edition, 2001), by Jeremy Gibson and Mervyn Medlycott.

## Street directories

Street or trade directories were first established in Ireland with the publication of Watson's *Gentleman and Citizen's Almanac* in Dublin in 1728. Since then, a range of publications have been produced elsewhere on the island at various points, with the first to appear in Limerick in 1769, and the first in Belfast in 1805. Some were published annually, and others far more infrequently, but the most notable publication runs include Wilson's *Dublin directories*, Thom's *Irish Almanacs*, Pettigrew and Oulston's *Almanacs*, James Pigot's and Isaac Slater's offerings, Smyth and Lyons' directories for Belfast, and directories from the Post Office.

Earlier directories tend to name only the great and the good, notably from the landed gentry, the clergy and the principal merchants, but over time, as the cities and population grew throughout the nineteenth century, the pool from which they recorded names and addresses expanded substantially. Whilst the earlier publications may simply provide an alphabetic list of inhabitants, the publications became considerably more sophisticated, with alphabetical listings, listings by streets, and then listings by trade or occupations all appearing within the same volume. Advertising also became an important feature, and many of the nineteenth-century adverts were elaborately designed, in some cases with etchings of the premises for particular businesses concerned.

In addition to information on people, many directories also include some useful gems for land-based research, with many providing an introductory overview of the region for which the book is concerned.

If we take a look at the Belfast Directory from 1831 to 1832 on the PRONI website, for example, which runs to some sixty-one pages, we find that immediately after the frontispiece there is *A Table of the Reciprocal Distances of Sixty-One of the Principal Towns in Ireland with the Distance from each other and of each from Dublin*, followed by a transcription of the Charter of Belfast granted to the town in 1613, in the reign of James VI & I. There is then a list of the streets to be featured in the directory, followed by a written breakdown of each of the districts of Belfast, and a description of the streets located within them. At the rear of the guide, following the alphabetical listing of people to be found in Belfast, and establishment information such as the names of societies, hospitals, jurors, churches etc., the book ends with a detailed travel supplement entitled *A Guide to the Giant's Causeway*. This is essentially a travel guide for those wishing to visit the attraction from Belfast, providing some observations on the towns and villages that would be encountered en route.

Copies of directories can be found all over Ireland in various archives and repositories, with large collections to be found in particular at the National Library of Ireland and the National Archives of Ireland, as well as at Belfast Central Library, and at PRONI. Shane Wilson's Irish Directory Database at **www.swilson.info/dirdb.php** provides links to over a thousand such resources which are hosted online. Many of these are dedicated collections, others just fragments from resources pertaining to a single area.

For Northern Ireland, the PRONI website offers a substantial digitised collection which can be freely searched by name and also browsed a page at a time. There are thirty volumes available, primarily for both Belfast and the province of Ulster between 1819 and 1900, as well as the 1839 edition of the *New Directory of the City of Londonderry and Coleraine, including Strabane with Lifford, Newtownlimavady, Portstewart and Portrush* and the 1840 *New Commercial Directory of Armagh, Newry, Londonderry, Drogheda, Dundalk, Monaghan, Omagh, Strabane, Dungannon, Lisburn, Lurgan, Portadown and neighbouring towns*.

Complementing this collection are two other fairly large online offerings. The Lennon Wylie website at **www.lennonwylie.co.uk**, courtesy of Mary Lennon, has transcribed directories listings for Belfast from 1805–1808, 1819, 1824, 1843, 1852, 1861, 1868, 1877, 1880, 1890, 1894, 1901, 1907–1910, 1912, 1918, 1924, 1932, 1939, 1943, 1947, 1951 and 1960. There is also a transcribed directory for Newry from 1898, for Waterford in 1894, and telephone directories for Belfast, Cork and Dublin from 1903 to 1904 and 1913. The 'Assorted Years' section is very specialised, listing pages from directories covering just a handful of streets in Belfast right up to 1970, but also worth a look if you have connections to the city. A fun page on the site at **www.lennonwylie.co.uk/funnynames.htm** lists strange, funny and wonderful names from the directories.

*Street directories can help to identify the tenants of properties beyond the census years.*

Elsewhere, the North of Ireland Family History Society's collection of directories from 1890 to 1947 is available on Findmypast through its 'Ireland, Belfast & Ulster Directories' collection. The volumes included are predominantly *The Belfast and Province of Ulster Directory*, and from 1923 onwards, The Belfast and Ulster Directory (which excluded coverage from this point for counties Cavan, Donegal and Monaghan).

Findmypast also offers additional directories for the whole of Ireland, which can be found by first selecting 'Directories & Social History' in the search menu, and making sure that returns from Ireland are selected, as opposed to Britain. The individual publication titles can be chosen through the sub-heading marked 'Directories and Almanacs'. Amongst the directories are several editions of the all-Ireland-based *Slater's National Directory* for 1846, 1870, 1881 and 1894, as well as provincial guides and other sources for cities such as Sligo, Waterford, Limerick, Cork and Dublin.

Many volumes for counties Clare, Galway, Limerick, Mayo and Roscommon can be found at **http://celticcousins.net/ireland**, whilst editions for Waterford from 1824, 1839, 1846, 1856, 1877, 1881, 1894 and 1909–10 are available in a database at **http://waterfordlibraries.ie/trade-directories/**. These also contain some records for Kilkenny, Tipperary, and the south-east of Ireland. For County Clare, visit **www.clarelibrary.ie/eolas/coclare/genealogy/genealog.htm** for offerings from 1788 to 1893.

Ancestry has very little street directory material for Ireland (an exception being *Thom's Directory* from 1904), though there are some other interesting inclusions. The site's 'U.K. and U.S. Directories, 1680–1830' collection contains 157 subscription lists for publications printed in Dublin in the eighteenth century. A few listings from some early nineteenth-century commercial directories are also included. An early 'directory' from Dublin, dated to 1647–1706, is also available from Dublin City Council at **https://databases.dublincity.ie/1647/about. php**. It includes the names of citizens compiled from various sources, including cess payments, noting the parish or street where they resided, their trade or occupation (if stated), and the payments of taxes or fines if stated.

## Electoral records

For much of Ireland's history before the union the general public did not have a vote, and democracy was predominantly the privilege of the Protestant landed classes. From 1727, only those Protestant freeholders holding land valued at 40 shillings were entitled to vote, but this right was extended by the Catholic Relief Act of 1793 to Roman Catholic freeholders with land held to the same value. This changed in 1829 when, following Catholic emancipation, the rate for freeholders was escalated to an annual rate of £10, stripping the rights away from many Protestants and Catholics alike. The net effect was to concentrate electoral power in the hands of the growing Protestant Ascendancy.

The absence of a secret ballot until 1872 was a situation open to abuse, and newspapers are full of accounts of tenants being penalised for voting against the wishes of their landlords. On 28 August 1826, for example, the *Dublin Morning Register* reported a meeting of a new Catholic Association in favour of emancipation. At the meeting, an incident in County Monaghan was recounted from the recent general election, whereby landlord Evelyn John Shirley had sought to influence the votes of his predominantly Roman Catholic tenantry:

There was another district of the County called the Barony of Farney – it was forfeited in the reign of Elizabeth, and had been for a long time in the possession of family of one Mr. Shirley, an Englishman, who was little known in this country. Mr. Shirley two or three years ago came to reside in Ireland, and although he professed liberal principles, he formed a political alliance with Colonel Leslie, a man who had been long odious in the eyes of the Catholics – he called upon his Catholic tenantry not merely to vote for him, but to give their second vote to Colonel Leslie, the head of the Orange party in the North.

The 'Colonel Leslie' in question here was Charles Powell Leslie, who had been an MP in Monaghan since Ireland had joined the UK in 1801, and a colonel of the Monaghan Militia. Whilst Shirley's Roman Catholic tenantry declined to take up his most interesting proposal to vote for the head of the Orange Society, they nevertheless did not wish to vote against their own landlord as a candidate.

> The election came on, the power of the Orange party appeared in all its insolence and all its force – the Catholics saw that they had an opportunity of getting rid of the head of that party, and accordingly almost every Catholic voted against Leslie, but every Catholic voted for Shirley...
>
> Accordingly, every man that could be influenced in that interest did vote for Mr. Shirley, and that gentleman was returned principally through the zeal of his tenants, by an overwhelming majority. Now, mark the return which Mr. Shirley made to his friends for having placed him in Parliament. The very next week he and his agents commenced an attack upon those very men. Not satisfied with the payment of the accustomed gale of rent, he called upon them for a dead or hanging gale, which they had never before been called upon to pay, and which he knew they were not able to pay. He had their cattle impounded, and set up to auction.

Fortunately for the tenants, nobody would buy the impounded animals, which were soon restored to them upon payment of their rents, with assistance from relief payments raised by the new Catholic Association. The full story is detailed in Martin Cahill's article 'The 1826 General Election in County Monaghan', within the *Clogher Record*, Vol. 5, No. 2 (1964), pp. 161–183, accessible via JSTOR (**www.jstor.org**).

As noted earlier, following Catholic emancipation in 1829, the property qualification for voters was increased to at least £10 for freeholders, disenfranchising many who previously held land at 40 shillings of value (i.e. £2). Thanks to the Representation of the People Act in 1832, the voting qualification was extended to £10 for freeholders, but also to holders of leases for lives (p.107), and to those who held leaseholds for sixty years.

An interesting consequence of the 1832 Act was the creation of a parliamentary Fictitious Votes Committee, concerned with fraudulent voter registration. The published *Reports from Committees, Fictitious Votes (Ireland), Select Committee on Fictitious Votes, 1837–1838* contains names from some 52,600 people so registered between 1832 and 1837 (most notably for Dublin). The collection is found on Findmypast, where it is entitled 'Ireland, Select Committee On Fictitious Votes 1837–1838', with an explanatory guide to the areas it contains records for detailed by the company's Irish team at **https://web.archive.org/web/20210120110054/https://www.findmypast. ie/articles/world-records/full-list-of-the-irish-family-history-records/ census-land-and-substitutes/reports-from-committees-fictitious-votes-ireland-select-committee-on-fictitious-votes-1837-1838**.

The original published editions from the *Select Committee on Fictitious Votes Ireland* can also be found freely on the Internet Archive, and include much of the evidence presented by those interviewed. Further information on the Fictitious Votes Committee can be found within the House of Commons Parliamentary Papers, which will also list freeholders from various areas in various reports and discussions from 1801 to 1922. The information can be found on the ProQuest hosted House of Commons Parliamentary Papers website (accessible via subscribing institutions), or the DIPPAM website at **www.dippam.ac.uk**, which includes the free-to-access 'Enhanced British Parliamentary Papers on Ireland' (EPPI) collection.

Findmypast also has a database entitled 'Ireland, Electoral Registers 1885–1886', which contains electoral registers from some twelve counties: Armagh, Fermanagh, Down, Limerick, Mayo, Meath, Tyrone, Roscommon, Westmeath, Wexford and Wicklow.

For Ulster, a selection of poll books from 1710 to 1840, showing who was eligible to vote or how they voted, has been made available on the PRONI website. PRONI also hosts the 1918 Absent Voters Lists from Counties Armagh and Londonderry, naming people engaged in war service who were eligible to vote, including members of the armed forces, the Merchant Navy, and those serving with the Red Cross and similar organisations.

For more recent electoral registers, listing those entitled to vote, there are collections held at the National Archives of Ireland, the NLI, and PRONI, but they are incomplete. Consult the catalogues for their respective holdings.

Dublin City registers from 1908 to 1915 are searchable online at **https:// databases.dublincity.ie**, whilst further rolls from 1937 to 1964 can be searched via databases in the Dublin City Library and Archive on Pearse Street. A complete set of Northern Irish registers from 1947 onwards is held also at the British Library in London, as well as registers for some earlier years.

## Newspapers

Newspapers can provide an exceptionally rich seam for our ancestors and their holdings. At their most basic, the intimations columns can simply confirm the presence of a person at a particular address at a certain time, but they can also add considerably more to our understanding of our ancestors' past holdings, and the context in which they held them within their local communities.

I previously mentioned the extensive newspaper coverage for my Bill family in the Templepatrick area in County Antrim (p.68), but the earliest article that I have so far found for this family's presence there comes from an advertisement noted in the *Belfast Newsletter* of 13 December 1768:

> To be let for 21 Years, or as such a term shall be agreed on, from the 1st May 1769, the following Lands in the County of Antrim, being Part of the Estate of Clotworthy Upton, Esq, viz:
>
> ...
>
> BALLYMARTIN
>
> ...
>
> John Bill 9 acres, 3 roods, 23 perches

This advert provided a long list of tenancies on the Upton estate which were up for renewal, with John Bill just one of those named as an already resident tenant on a plot comprising 9 acres, 3 roods and 23 perches (p.43). However, this particular advert also led to a storm of protests, with the landlord offering no security of tenure and a massive increase in rents, driving many previous tenants off their lands as a consequence. John successfully maintained his tenancy, but this was not looked upon well by his neighbours, who saw him as complicit in the situation. A follow up news report on 25 July 1769 notes what happened next:

> WHEREAS in the Night of the 13th of July Instant, some wicked and malicious Person or Persons did feloniously set on fire the Out-houses belonging to John Bill of Ballymartin, near Templepatrick in the County of Antrim, in which were sundry Things of Value, which together with the Houses, were burned down and consumed to Ashes.
>
> And on the night of the 21st Instant, some such wicked Persons did feloniously stab and maim a Cow belonging to the said John Bill.

In this following example, a notice from the *Northern Constitution* on 19 September 1896 advertised a forthcoming auction of household possessions commissioned by my three times great-grandfather William Watton, in advance of his relocation from Portstewart to Belfast, providing a wonderful overview of his holdings, and an insight into his social standing:

AUCTION OF HOUSEHOLD FURNITURE, HORSE, CAR, CART & HARNESS,
AT MAIN STREET, PORTSTEWART

To be Sold by Public Auction, at MAIN STREET, PORTSTEWART, on TUESDAY, 22nd September, commencing at Eleven o'clock, the following property of Mr. William Watton (who is removing):-

IN PARLOUR – 6 Baloon Back [*sic*] Chairs, 1 Mahogany Cabinet, 1 Lady's Arm Chair, 1 Square Birch Table, 1 Duplex Lamp, 1 Gent's Arm Chair, 1 Couch, Carpet and Earth Rug, 1 Side Table, 1 Gilt Mantel Mirror, 1 Whatnot, and 5 Pictures.

IN HALL – 1 Clock (8-day), 2 Chairs, 1 Table, 1 Picture.
The entire Furniture and Appointments of Four Bedrooms, comprising Iron and other Bedsteads, Spring and Flock Mattresses, Feather Beds, Blankets, Quilts, Pillows, Bolsters, Wardrobes, Dressing Tables, Looking Glasses, Wash Stand, Towel Rails, Bedroom Ware, Pictures, Carpets, Mahogany Couch, Tables, &c., &c.

MISCELLANEOUS EFFECTS – 1 Singer's Sewing Machine, 1 Patent Mangel [*sic*] (Williamson & Co.), 1 good Posting Horse, Car, Cart and Harness, all and singular the entire Kitchen Utensils, Glass, and China.

Terms – Cash, and Fees.
J. F. GLENN & CO., Auctioneers, Coleraine

A subsequent article in the *Derry Journal* from 25 September in fact added considerably more drama to the proceedings, describing how a young woman called Sarah Hutchinson had collapsed whilst attending this auction, and subsequently died, with an inquest noting this to be from natural causes.

In times of tragedy, newspapers can also really help to bring things to life with our ancestral homesteads. An extraordinary article from the *Munster Express* of 20 July 1934 relates an incident which took place at the farm of Thomas Prendergast during the Civil War. Thomas was first cousin of my wife's grandfather, and his farm was in fact the Prendergast family home for well over a century before that. In the summer of 1922, at the farm of Killonerry, parish of Whitechurch, County Kilkenny, a dramatic three-day skirmish took place between the Free State Army and those opposed to the Anglo-Irish Treaty, for which Thomas made a compensation claim twelve years later for £107 17s 3d for damage done to the farm building:

Applicant said that he was an active sympathiser with the I.R.A. and then his sympathies went to those who opposed the Free State forces after the Treaty. He was actually out driving for them. He was advised by his solicitors not to apply for compensation under the 1923 Act. He was not at home in July or August. He was there some time previous to July and the damage for which he now claimed compensation was not then done. The Irregular troops were encamped at a wood by a tributary of the Suir near his house. Col. Prout and the Free State troops came up from Waterford and there was a three days battle during which the Free State troops occupied the house. Applicant was arrested on the day they arrived and kept in an outhouse. He found all this damage when he came back. He was claiming for repairs to the floor, joists, windows, skirting, plastering etc. Applicant had got an estimate for repairs from a Carrick-on-Suir firm. He had deducted 60 per cent from the estimate for joinery because he admitted the woodwork in the house was old at the time. In the case of the plastering he had deducted 50 per cent. There were also certain articles taken away by the troops – an overcoat, suits of clothes and pairs of boots. He had paid £10 for the two suits of clothes and regarded them being worth half price at the time they were taken. He was also claiming half price in respect of some shirts. He was claiming £3 for a mahogany dining table, and he was also claiming for a mahogany washstand, four mahogany chairs, mattresses, covers, quilts. Practically all the delph and china in the house was broken. He claimed £5 for this item, as well as £1 10s. for mechanic's tools. Other articles taken included two razors and three pairs of lace curtains out of which the troops made stockings (laughter).

*The two Prendergast farms at Killonerry townland, site of a civil war battle in 1922.*

In the same article, my wife's great-grandfather, also called Thomas Prendergast, confirmed the damage to his nephew's property, but noted further damage carried out on his own adjacent farm, with the slaughter of his cattle by the Free State Army:

> Thomas Prendergast, uncle of the applicant, said he lived near Kilonery [*sic*] House, and saw the troops breaking out the windows in July or August, 1922. The various articles for which applicant claimed compensation were in the house before the Free State troops occupied it. He saw the house afterwards and it was a teetotal wreck. 'In fact,' said witness, 'myself was worth it.'
>
> Mr. Budd – You were a total wreck too?
> Witness – They killed all my cattle.
> Did you get compensation? – I did.

Compensation was subsequently paid out to the value of £102, with an additional £3 for expenses.

Newspapers can be found in many archival institutions, but much of the credit behind the opening up of such an important resource to researchers in recent years must go to both the British Library and to the National Library of Ireland. Between the 1980s and the early part of the twenty-first century, the two national libraries collaborated on the NEWSPLAN project (and its successor, NEWSPLAN 2000), to catalogue and make available on microfilm a range of titles from across the island of Ireland. The results of this cataloguing effort can now be accessed on the National Library's website at **www.nli.ie/en/newspapers-catalogues-and-databases.aspx**, through the library's 'Newspaper Database', which allows you to search for titles held across the whole island of Ireland, north and south, including some titles that were published beyond Ireland's shores.

Located at **www.nli.ie/en/catalogues-and-databases-printed-newspapers. aspx**, the database permits user to search by the name of a title, a town or city, or by county. A search for 'Sligo', for example, will reveal nineteen titles for the town and county held at the library. Exploring the results then gives me more information – if I click on the *Sligo Independent*, it tells me that the paper was known as the *Sligo Independent* from 29 September 1855 to September 1921, and then as the *Sligo Independent and West of Ireland Advertiser* until it ceased publication in 1961. It also identifies which issues are held on microfilm, and which as hard copies.

If I now repeat the search but click on the option marked 'Include titles from the NEWSPLAN project not held by the NLI', I discover twenty titles listed in the return, instead of fifteen. Although the NLI holds the *Sligo Chronicle* from 1851– 22 April 1893, it turns out that Sligo County Library holds copies of a separate newspaper of the same name, which ran from 1896–99, and which cannot be accessed in Dublin.

There are two huge online platforms which offer worthwhile starting points for newspaper research. The Irish Newspaper Archives (**www. irishnewsarchive.com**) contains many digitised titles, mainly from the Republic, though with some from Northern Ireland. Its most historic title is the *Belfast Newsletter*, which commenced publication from 1737, making it the oldest English language newspaper in the world still being published, and for which the archive holds a complete run from 1738 onwards. Of the many titles available on the Irish Newspaper Archives, additional significant holdings include the *Irish Independent*, the *Freeman's Journal*, *The Nation*, the *Anglo-Celt*, the *Connaught Tribune*, the *Munster Express*, and the *Belfast Telegraph*. The site is subscription-based, although institutional access is offered by some subscribing libraries across the world.

The British Newspaper Archive (**www.britishnewspaperarchive. co.uk**) also hosts a significant amount of content for Ireland, much of which can also be accessed via Findmypast (**www.findmypast.com**). This project is a collaboration between Findmypast and the British Library, and already hosts more than the target 40 million pages of content which the project sought to place online. Within a UK context, Ireland also features in many titles which have originated in Britain itself. Note that this is still but a drop in the ocean compared to the complete holdings of the British Library's Newspaper Library at Boston Spa, Yorkshire (**www.bl.uk/visit/reading-rooms/boston-spa**).

Whilst it is certainly a game changer that so many records can be viewed online now, there are some issues to be wary of when using newspaper databases. Such platforms utilise Optical Character Recognition (OCR) to scan text from original content, sometimes from within bound volumes, and this can struggle at times with print at very small size, or on the curve as the page turns into the spine of a bound volume, meaning some items can be missed on a search – you may find ten references to a John Smith, for example, when fifteen actually exist. Also note older conventions, such as the use of apostrophes instead of small 'c' (McMillan printed as M'Millan), and the old form letter 's', which may be read as an 'f'. Another key issue, and one which you may also encounter when using newspaper microfilms, is that within some titles there may be more than one edition published in a single day, with revised content – particularly on a Saturday when the sports results came in and the news went out of the window!

The state-based *Gazettes* include further announcements that can be useful for house history and land research, including business partnership announcement, bankruptcies, notifications on probate situations, and planning permission applications. Prior to Partition the state paper for the whole of Ireland was the *Dublin Gazette*, which existed from 1706 to 1921. The largest available collection online, covering the period from 1750 to 1800, is freely available from the Irish Parliament's Oireachtas Library website at **https://opac.oireachtas.ie**. These are presented in hefty-sized PDF files of about 1GB each, covering about a year each, which can be viewed online or freely downloaded. Findmypast also offers a database providing access to this collection, entitled 'Ireland, Dublin Gazette 1750–1800'.

Following Partition, the *Dublin Gazette* was replaced in the Republic with *Iris Ofigiúil*. Editions are unfortunately only online from 2002 onwards at **www.irisoifigiuil.ie**, although a handful of earlier articles are digitised and available on the Oireachtas Library website. In the north, the *Belfast Gazette* commenced publication from 7 June 1921 as the official newspaper of state for Northern Ireland. All editions are freely available at **www.thegazette.co.uk**. As will be noted later (p.136), the *Belfast Gazette* can be extremely useful for searching for property sales after Partition.

Local studies libraries and archives are equally worth checking for holdings on site and online. Several titles have been digitised by

Waterford City and County Libraries and made freely available online in 'browse only' format at **www.waterfordcouncil.ie/departments/library/local-newspapers.htm**, including the *Dungarvan Leader* (1943–2007), the *Dungarvan Observer* (1918–79) and the *Waterford Chronicle* (1811–72). Where titles have not been digitised, information on local holdings can still be found. Cavan's county library, for example, offers a guide at **www.cavanlibrary.ie/Default.aspx?StructureID_str=32**, Cork Past and Present has a list at **www.corkpastandpresent.ie/localstudies/newspaperlist/**, whilst Tipperary Studies offers a similar platform noting details of its collections at **https://tipperarystudies.ie/newspapers**.

The largest collection of newspaper holdings for Northern Ireland can be consulted at Belfast Central Library's Newspaper Library. Its website at **www.librariesni.org.uk/resources/cultural-heritage/cultural-heritage-collections/belfast-central-library/newspaper-library-belfast-central-library/** offers a list of titles available for consultation. PRONI also offers several titles on microfilm in Belfast, with a guide to these available at **www.nidirect.gov.uk/publications/newspapers-available-microfilm**.

# Chapter 5

# VALUATION SURVEYS

Since the seventeenth century, many national exercises have been carried out to determine the size, boundaries and valuation of land across Ireland. Much of the material available to us is original documentation that was never at risk from the Public Record Office fire in 1922, due to it being stored elsewhere, whilst other resources are early transcriptions and copies made for official purposes, which can compensate for original material which was lost.

Valuation records from the nineteenth century in particular can help to plug the gaps left by the loss of the decennial censuses, although a word of caution should be sounded. Despite such records being described by many as 'census substitutes', they were certainly not drawn up as censuses, and the earliest records often miss out many of those who held much smaller properties, due to the set criteria that were laid down for those carrying out the valuation work. Nevertheless, they are a massively important resource which can help to reveal a great deal of how the land was administered, and occupied.

## The Down Survey of Ireland

If you are able to trace your families back to the seventeenth century, an important land resource from that period can be found in the Down Survey of Ireland, which underpinned the establishment of the Protestant Ascendancy for the next two centuries.

Following the Tudor plantations of the mid-seventeenth century, the Hamilton-Montgomery settlements of 1606 in Antrim and Down, and the subsequent Plantations of Ulster from 1609, the native Irish Catholic population found themselves suddenly living in an occupied territory. Some were dispossessed, and retaliated through raids on the new settlers as bandits known as 'woodkerns'. Some limited conversions from

Catholicism to the new Protestant faith did occur, but most remained as adherents to their traditional faith. In 1641, as part of the lead up to the Wars of the Three Kingdoms (p.21), a rebellion by native Catholics took place in Ulster, with some 4,000 Protestants, Scottish and English, killed, and many thousands more forced to flee. Some 8,000 testimonies gathered in subsequent years from many of those who witnessed the massacre are held by Trinity College Dublin and reveal a great deal about the early stages of the Plantations. These can be viewed online freely at **https://1641.tcd.ie**.

Following the subsequent Cromwellian conquest of Ireland, the English Parliament's Act of Settlement in 1652 decreed which lands in Ireland were to be forfeited by Catholic landowners who had participated in the 1641 rebellion, as well as Catholic clergy, royalists, and anyone who had directed hostilities against the English army. The intent was to convey their holdings to loyal English soldiers for service and to 'Adventurers' or speculators for their investment in the conflict, with many of the dispossessed Catholics affected forcibly transplanted to the province of Connacht.

To prepare for the mass forfeiture, Cromwell ordered a Civil Survey to be carried out from 1654 to 1656 to value land across the four provinces (although most of Connacht had already been surveyed in an earlier exercise from 1630). With the aid of this information, Sir William Petty was tasked with carrying out the more accurate Down Survey from 1656 to 1658, with the word 'Down' in this context having nothing to do with the county, but with the set length chains that were 'put down' to measure each townland in the country. The survey, and the accompanying maps generated, were the first attempt to accurately map the island of Ireland, with the map recorded at a scale of 40 perches to the inch.

Following the Restoration, 'Books of Survey and Distribution' were created from this earlier exercise. These were used by the Quit Rent Office (p.115) to levy the 'quit rent' tax due by landholders, and were collated by barony, and then by parish. Many copies of these books were created, with a useful summary outlined by the Royal Irish Academy at **www.ria.ie/books-survey-and-distribution**, which itself holds a collection of sixteen bound volumes. Additional collections are held by the National Archives of Ireland, the NLI, and at PRONI.

Various published volumes of the Books of Survey and Distribution, and from the Civil Survey, can be accessed in digital format via the Irish Manuscripts Commission website at **www.irishmanuscripts.ie**, as follows:

The Civil Survey A.D. 1654–1656:
- Vol. I. County of Tipperary – Eastern & Southern Baronies
- Vol. II. County of Tipperary – Western & Northern Baronies
- Vol. III. Counties of Donegal, Londonderry and Tyrone
- Vol. IV. County of Limerick with a section of Clanmaurice barony Co. Kerry
- Vol. V. County of Meath
- Vol. VI. County of Waterford – Muskerry barony Co. Cork; Kilkenny City and Liberties (part); also valuations *c.* 1663–64 for Waterford and Cork cities
- Vol. VII. County of Dublin
- Vol. VIII. county of Kildare
- Vol. IX. County of Wexford
- Vol. X. Miscellanea

Topographical index of the parishes and townlands of Ireland in Sir William Petty's MSS barony maps (*c.* 1655–9) and Hiberniae Delineatio (*c.* 1672)

Books of Survey and Distribution being abstracts of various surveys and instruments of title 1636–1703:

- Vol. I. County of Roscommon with maps *c.* 1636 of the baronies of Athlone and Moycarnan and of parishes in Ballintober
- Vol. II. County of Mayo with maps of the county from Petty's Atlas 1683 and of Tirawley barony from the Down Survey 1657

*Digitised copies of the Books of Survey and Distribution are hosted on the Irish Manuscripts Commission website.*

- Vol. III. County of Galway with map of the county from Petty's Atlas 1683
- Vol. IV. County of Clare reproduced from the manuscript in the Public Record Office of Ireland with maps

Although the original Down Survey was destroyed in a Dublin fire in 1711, it has been faithfully reconstructed using contemporary copies and placed online by Trinity College Dublin at **http://downsurvey.tcd. ie**, along with the Books of Survey and Distribution, which can be freely consulted. There are two main areas worth plundering on the site:

1. The 'Down Survey Maps' section hosts maps created at four levels – for the island of Ireland, the counties, the baronies, and the civil parishes – which are accompanied by 'terriers' or written descriptions of the areas involved.
2. The 'Historical GIS' section allows you to identify information about the ownership of specific townlands in 1641 and 1670, as noted in copies of the Books of Survey and Distribution as originally held by the Quit Rent Office in Dublin (p.115). Helpfully, the inclusion of nineteenth-century Ordnance Survey maps helps to locate townlands

*The Down Survey of Ireland website.*

of interest in the earlier maps. You can identify the holdings of individual landowners, the make-up of an area by its religious denomination, and also plot where individual murders from the earlier 1641 Irish Rebellion occurred (p.65).

If I search for the townland of Lisnisk in the County Antrim parish of Ballyrashane within the Historical GIS section, I can easily locate it to the west of the town of Coleraine using the nineteenth-century Ordnance Survey map. Once I have zoomed in to the maximum, the borders of individual townlands appear, and by clicking on the area where Lisnisk is located I receive the following information in a small pop-up window:

Townland of Lisnisk

| | |
|---|---|
| Down Survey Name: | Carneglasse |
| 1641 Owner(s): | Macdonnell, Randal Earl of Antrim (Catholic) |
| 1670 Owner(s): | McFedderish, William (Catholic) County: Antrim |
| Barony: | Dunluce |
| Parish: | Ballyrashan [sic] |
| Unprofitable land: | 108 plantation acres |
| Profitable land: | 396 plantation acres |

The names of Randall MacDonnell (Earl of Antrim) and William McFedderish are both presented as hyperlinks, and by clicking on these I can now find more information about their total landholdings at this time. Starting with MacDonnell in 1641, he was noted as having 929 townland holdings in County Antrim, 56 in Derry and 4 in Tyrone. MacDonnell was in fact the 2nd Earl of Antrim, and a fervent Royalist, whose lands were seized during the Cromwellian settlement; it was not until 1666, following the Restoration of Charles II, that his lands in Dunluce and Glenarm were returned to his possession. As can be seen in 1670, however, Lisnisk was not amongst these, which is instead now shown as being held by a William McFedderish. Upon a similar investigation, we see that he held just thirteen townlands in and around Lisnisk, and no lands at all in 1641.

## Tithe records

As the state church, the Church of Ireland derived income from several sources. Prior to 1833 it could charge a cess for its various parochial activities, and it also held lands on which it could derive rents from tenants. One of its largest forms of income, however, was a payment due from parishioners of a tithe, or one tenth of any produce generated, for the upkeep of its clergy, although some of the payments went instead to landowners and to the Crown.

In the early nineteenth century, the decision was taken to have all such payments made in monetary form, and not in kind as had been customary up to that point. The Composition for Tithes (Ireland) Act of 1823 was set up to work out the value of such tithes payments, and its records therefore act as a useful resource in describing the size of land holdings and the heads of the households occupying them. Not all lands are included, with omissions for property owned by the Church, for land that had little rateable value due to poor quality, or for land beyond the Church's parochial jurisdiction.

The set tithe was fiercely objected to, being deemed to be horrendously unfair in its application, with the poor often paying the most. Many people refused to pay, thereby 'defaulting'. A list of defaulters from 1831 can be found on Findmypast (p.14), with names from Carlow, Cork, Kerry, Kilkenny, Laois, Limerick, Louth, Meath, Offaly, Tipperary, Waterford and Wexford, whilst the 'Report from the Select Committee on the Tithes in Ireland from 1831 to 1832' can be consulted with the papers of the House of Commons (p.74), which contain many interviews with people experiencing issues in the collection of the tax.

Despite attempts at reform, a huge change was finally implemented in 1838 with the Tithe Rentcharge Act, which reduced the charge by a quarter and allowed it to be collected as part of the standard rents due to landlords. Despite the payments no longer going to the Church of Ireland following its disestablishment in 1871, it was still deemed to be a tax, which continued to be paid to the Irish Land Commission (p.131).

The tithe applotment records for the Republic of Ireland, which include some cross-border areas in the north, have been digitised and made freely available online via **www.genealogy.nationalarchives.ie**. They can be searched for by an individual name (forename and/or surname), county, civil parish and townland, or browsed by county and civil parish. The images, presented in black and white, can be downloaded and saved in PDF format to your computer.

When carrying out a search for a name in the database, the last column returned notes the year between 1823 and 1837 in which the record was compiled, but it is sometimes possible to glean the exact date itself from additional documents included with the tithes books. Although not immediately obvious, these records from the microfilms have been digitised, but cannot be searched for using the search fields – however, they can be accessed online.

There are a couple of ways to locate these records. First, you can view the documents by manipulating the URL (website address) to step through subsequent pages on the digital microfilm (e.g. change the last three numbers at the end of **http://titheapplotmentbooks.nationalarchives. ie/reels/tab//004625725/004625725_00288.pdf** (page 288) to **http:// titheapplotmentbooks.nationalarchives.ie/reels/tab//004625725/0046 25725_00289.pdf** (page 289), and onwards).

A much easier way to determine this information, and to view these additional pages, is to search for the same records through the FamilySearch database entitled 'Ireland Tithe Applotment Books, 1814–1855'. In any search return, a transcription at the bottom of the page will include the year of the 'tax assessment' given, and you can step through the images of the full digital microfilm using arrows beside the 'Image' box showing the number of the page currently being viewed.

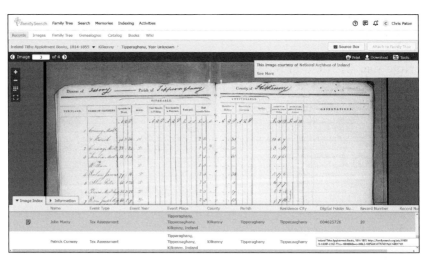

*The tithe applotment books for the Republic of Ireland can be easily searched on the FamilySearch platform.*

Northern records can also be consulted at the National Archives in Dublin on microfilm, whilst some have been indexed on Ancestry (p.14), albeit incompletely. Microfilm copies for all of Ulster's nine counties can be consulted at PRONI, along with the original records for the six Northern Ireland counties, with a name index for those liable to pay the tithe available on microfilm series MIC/15K.

However, in late 2019 the digitised records for the six Northern Ireland counties were made available by PRONI through its online catalogue, in full colour and at a very high resolution. The records can only be browsed at present, but PRONI staff are working on a name index which will be made available at some future stage.

The Northern Irish books can be viewed or downloaded for parishes as follows:

- From the PRONI home page at **www.nidirect.gov.uk/proni**, click on the eCatalogue link
- Click on Search PRONI's eCatalogue
- Scroll down and click on the green Search the eCatalogue button
- On the top right of the catalogue search screen, click Browse
- Type in FIN/5/A and click on Search
- On the results page, click on the FIN/5/A hyperlink beside the second option, Tithe Applotment Records for Parishes in Northern Ireland
- You will be taken to a detailed listing for each civil parish in alphabetical order
- The View link at the end column allows you to view or download a PDF file of the record

Note that the PDF files are very large, and you may find it easier to download them and view with an internet browser rather than with a PDF reader.

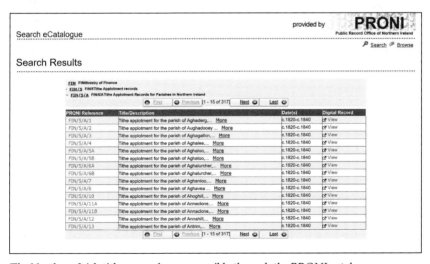

*The Northern Irish tithes records are accessible through the PRONI catalogue.*

## Townland Valuation

Estate owners would occasionally carry out surveys of their property to determine its rateable value, often with a view to improving their income. Surviving records may be found in estate papers' collections (p.100). However, the state itself also had a vested interest in knowing the value of land across the country, and in the nineteenth century carried out two important national valuations.

Following the passage of the Valuation of Land (Ireland) Act 1826, from 1828 to 1840 a nationwide Townland Valuation was commenced by Boundary Commissioner Richard John Griffith, for properties with an annual rateable value of £3, which increased to £5 from 1838. These include details of ownership, but due to the values of the properties that were targeted it tends to be more useful for the records of urban residents than those living in the rural parts of the country.

Records from the Valuation Office are catalogued by the NAI under the letters OL, the abbreviation of its Gaelic name, *Oifig Luachála*. The field work for the Townland Valuation, which is now online, will be discussed shortly, but appeals against the valuation were permitted under the 1826 Act, with materials surviving from this held at the NAI under OL/13. Following the appeals, the Townland Valuation returns were published over a series of twenty-six volumes between 1836 and 1850, with a full set available at the NLI, whilst the NAI holds twenty of the volumes. However, the names of occupiers and owners are not included within these books, which concentrate on the statistical information derived from the exercise.

The 'Report from the Select Committee on Townland Valuation of Ireland', published in 1844, can be read at the Internet Archive at **https://archive.org/details/op1246071-1001**. It concluded that in the aftermath of the Poor Relief (Ireland) Act of 1838, the Townland Valuation could not be utilised for the administration of the poor rate or the county cess, paving the way for a subsequent, and more inclusive, Tenement Valuation (p.91).

## Valuation field work

The field work carried out by Griffith's team for both the Townland Valuation, and the subsequent Tenement Valuation, was recorded in a series of manuscript books, which are digitised and now available on the NAI's genealogy platform at **www.genealogy.nationalarchives.ie** and **http://census.nationalarchives.ie/search/vob/home.jsp**. Noted as the 'Valuation Office Books 1824–1856' collection, the collection comprises four main series of books:

1. **Field Books** were used to record information about agricultural holdings, and compiled by civil parish. They provide information on townlands as divided into 'lots' based on factors such as soil quality, and only list the names of lessors of property valued at £3 annually prior to 1844, and £5 after.

2. **House Books** primarily recorded information about urban areas, listing the names of occupiers of houses that were valued if they met the same valuation criteria, but some properties in rural areas were also included. They include details such as the names of occupiers, the 'quality' of the house (based on its manner of construction and state or repair), its physical dimensions and the valuation.

3. **Tenure Books** or **Perambulation Books** were notebooks recorded by staff visiting the properties from 1846 to 1858. No tenure books have survived for County Laois, but where books survive for other counties they often contain more information than the final published version of the Tenement Valuation. This includes the name of occupiers and immediate lessors, details about the annual rent, the year when a tenancy was let, and a description of the tenement.

4. **Quarto Books** were used to compile information about properties in towns from 1839 to 1851 or both the Townland and Tenement Valuations, based on information extracted from the House Books. None have survived for Counties Leitrim and Sligo, and only a handful of books exist for some of the other counties.

The detailed instructions given to the valuators in 1833, and again in 1844 and 1853, can be read on the NAI's 'Guide to the archives of the Valuation Office' page at **www.nationalarchives.ie/article/guide-archives-valuation-office** – scroll to the bottom of the page to find the following downloadable guides:

- OL/1/2/2    Instructions to valuators (1833)
- OL/1/2/6    Instructions to valuators (1844)
- OL/1/2/5    Additional instructions to valuators (1844)
- OL/1/2/7    Instructions to valuators (1853) part 1
- OL/1/2/7    Instructions to valuators (1853) part 2
- OL/1/2/7    Instructions to valuators (1853) part 3
- OL/1/2/7    Instructions to valuators (1853) part 4

### Tenement Valuation (Griffith's Valuation)
Following problems encountered with the data being made available from the Townland Valuation, particularly with regards to information

required to help fund the new poor law system in Ireland through local taxation from 1838, a subsequent nationwide Tenement Valuation from 1846 was established, with revised criteria, again led by Richard Griffith.

The results were published between 1847 and 1864 as the *Primary Valuation of Ireland*, more colloquially known as 'Griffith's Valuation', in the following years:

| Ulster | Munster | Connacht | Leinster |
|---|---|---|---|
| Antrim 1861–2 | Clare 1855 | Galway 1855 | Carlow 1852–3 |
| Armagh 1864 | Cork 1851–53 | Leitrim 1856 | Dublin 1848–51 |
| Cavan 1856–7 | Kerry 1852 | Mayo 1856–7 | Kildare 1851 |
| Derry 1858–9 | Limerick 1851–2 | Roscommon 1857–8 | Kilkenny 1849–50 |
| Donegal 1857 | Tipperary 1851 | Sligo 1858 | Laois 1851–2 |
| Down 1863–4 | Waterford 1848–51 | | Longford 1854 |
| Fermanagh 1862 | | | Louth 1854 |
| Monaghan 1858–60 | | | Meath 1855 |
| Tyrone 1851 | | | Offaly 1854 |
| | | | Westmeath 1854 |
| | | | Wexford 1853 |
| | | | Wicklow 1852–3 |

There are many sites offering access to transcripts or images of the Tenement Valuation as 'Griffith's Valuation', but by far the most user friendly is that at AskAboutIreland.ie (**www.askaboutireland.ie**). This site is not only free, it also offers copies of Ordnance Survey maps, albeit not quite contemporary, which in most cases can be used to plot the locations of all the properties recorded, with individual lot numbers marked out with red boundaries.

Findmypast hosts a more complete collection of the records, entitled 'Griffith's Valuation 1847–1864', which includes revisions after appeals (p.95), but on a subscription-based platform. The records are accompanied by a separate maps collection, 'Griffith's Survey Maps & Plans, 1847–1864', which is more contemporary with the original valuation, but with the maps presented in black and white, making it more difficult in many instances to make out the boundaries of lots.

On AskAboutIreland.ie you can perform an initial search by surname, forename, county, barony, union or parish, but not by townland (which you can do on Findmypast). The results page allows you to see a brief summary of the items returned for the search, and clicking on the 'Details' link will provide additional information such as the townland and street name, the landlord's details, and the all-important publication date. If I carry out a search for my great great-grandfather Jackson Curry, for example, the entry found shows that he lived in the townland

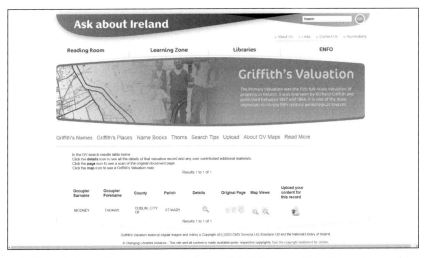

*Ask About Ireland offers free access to the published Primary Valuation returns, along with corresponding maps.*

of Lemnaroy, in the Londonderry parish of Termoneeny, and that his landlord was James McWhinney. The entry was published in 1859.

As well as this basic summary, you can then view the original document image for an entry by clicking on a link in the 'Original Page' menu heading. This will bring up a page from the published edition, with additional information given for Jackson under the following column headings:

| o. and Letters Reference to ap | Names | | Description of Tenement | Area | Rateable Annual Valuation | | Total Annual Valuation |
|---|---|---|---|---|---|---|---|
| | Streets, &c, & Occupiers | Immediate Lessors | | | Land | Buildings | of Rateable Property |
| | | | | | £. s. d. | £. s. d. | £. s. d. |
| LEMNAROY – continued Jackson Curry | James McWhinney | | House and Land | A. R. P. 7. 0. 0. | 3. 10. 0 | 0. 5. 0. | 3. 15. 0 |

In the left column is a reference number which can be used to then identify the lot on the accompanying marked up Ordnance Survey map, again accessible from the main menu through the 'Map Views' options. In this case I would be looking for the plot numbered 25 in the accompanying map of Lemnaroy townland, and once accessed, I can view the map (which may take a few moments to load up on to my screen) and use a control bar in the top right of the screen to mix through to a modern edition map showing the same area.

However, an issue to be aware of is that the main coloured maps presented as the default on AskAboutIreland are not quite contemporary with the valuation (instead dating from revaluation work up to twenty years later), and in some cases you may not find the holding in question. For areas in the Republic, it is possible to view alternative, undated, black and white maps on the AskAboutIreland site using the 'Map Version' controls in the top right corner of the screen. Although undated, the site does note that 'the earliest map versions are those in black and white sketch and the latest versions are those in coloured print'. If problems arise, the Findmypast collection of maps offers an alternative means to locate a property.

The map reference numbers given in the Griffith's returns can sometimes be a little more complicated to interpret than just a straightforward number, however, with additional letters appended to the number in both lower and upper case. A useful guide explaining how this system works is available at **www.askaboutireland.ie/reading-room/history-heritage/irish-genealogy/understanding-the-valuati/**.

In summary, the ordinal numbers given refer to the lot numbers i.e. the holdings as shown in the maps using red outlined boundaries. A lot may have been subdivided, in which case each portion will then have a capital letter after it. Buildings will be noted with an italicised lower case letter after.

Take for example a hypothetical situation in the following simplified extract:

| No. & Letters of Reference to Map | Occupier | Landlord's Name |
|---|---|---|
| 6 A *a* <br> – B | John Smith | *John Smith's landlord* |
| A *b* | Female Tenant 1 | John Smith |
| B *a* | Male Tenant 2 | John Smith |
| – *b* | Male Tenant 3 | John Smith |
| 7 | *Name of the next lot holder* | *His or her landlord* |

In this mythical example, lot 6 of a particular townland belongs to John Smith. He has two subdivisions in this lot, which are noted as A and B. he himself lives in subdivision A, hence the small italic *a* beside this. Below the entry for John's name, there are now entries for his tenants. In the subdivision marked A, there is a female tenant listed, with an italic *b* beside her name. This signifies that she lives in the same subdivision as her landlord, but in a different building. In the subdivision marked as B, there are two tenants. Again, they live in separate buildings in the subdivision, and so have an italic *a* and *b* beside them. Of course, it may not be quite so straightforward in all cases!

As with the tithes records, this was not a census. In addition to the name of the immediate lessor, the return will only show the name of the lessee, usually the person who was deemed to be the head of the household, and no-one else in the family. In some instances you may find the first name of a person's father in brackets after a tenant, if the tenant has the same name as someone else in the vicinity. With the exercise not carried out in every county at the same time (as with a census) it is also theoretically possible to find an ancestor recorded in two different counties for which the gathering of evidence and subsequent publication was not simultaneous.

If you are unable to find a person listed in a search, you can browse the records instead using the Griffith's Places menu option on AskAboutIreland.ie, which allows you to select an area by a place name search, or by selecting a barony, poor law union and/or parish from drop-down menu lists. On Findmypast you can more easily search by townland to obtain a list of inhabitants.

## Valuation appeals

Appeals to these later valuations were enabled under the Tenement Valuation Acts of 1846 and 1852, all taken under oath, for a variety of reasons. Many properties saw substantial changes in the intervening period between the gathering of the field work and the eventual publication, with new tenants, landlords, or the buildings involved amended or demolished. Others complained that the valuation of their lots was too high. The majority of the appeals concerned the holding of agricultural land.

A great deal of material is held at the NAI in Dublin for specific applications, including the appeal application books, and the original sub-commissioners' appeal books, which includes handwritten notes from oral testimonies given at the appeal, often noting many grievances from the appellant. These can include a great deal of information on genealogical relationships, rents paid, the nature of the properties involved, and local events which may have impacted, not least with this period being in the immediate aftermath of the Famine.

Surviving materials for appeals following the 1846 Act are held for some seventy-five baronies in counties Carlow, Clare, Dublin, Kerry (one document), Kildare, Kilkenny, Limerick, Tipperary, Waterford, Wicklow and Laois (Queen's County), catalogued under OL/19 and microfilms

MFA/16 and MFA/19. Some thirty-six books for the counties were also published between 1849 and 1851 with the revised valuations, whilst later revisions survive in manuscript form only at the NAI.

With the earlier appeals published, it is sometimes possible to find more than one entry for a property in the more complete online database for Griffith's Valuation on Findmypast. For example, in the original published return on 10 July 1850 for Killonerry townland in the parish of Whitechurch, Co. Kilkenny, my wife's great great-grandfather Thomas Prendergast was listed as the holder of just over 22 acres, held on a lease from a Robert Walsh Esquire, with the land having a rateable value of £26 10s. The number 8 in the left column of the published return corresponds with the markings on the survey map, and shows that Thomas held a portion of land to the far south-east corner of the townland. This did not correspond with the known location of the family farm, Killonerry House, in more recent times, and suggested there may have been more to the family's presence in the townland.

Shortly after the first publication, a second publication of the returns was produced on 30 December 1850 with an entry for Thomas 'as altered on appeal by the sub-commissioners'. In this we again find Thomas holding the same 22 acres, but this time from the Earl of Bessborough, not Robert Walsh, and with the rateable value reduced to £25 from £26 10s. In addition to this return, there was now a second holding of land listed for Thomas in the townland, marked as plot 4, which was substantially larger, at over 119 acres, and valued at £150. More importantly, this corresponded with the known location of the family farm, showing that earlier in the century the family had come from more humble origins, but had then substantially expanded their farming business in the townland, taking on the largest farm holding there. Without considering all of the documentation available from the Griffith's Valuation records, a substantial development within the family's story may well have been overlooked.

Later appeals from the counties heard under the 1846 Act were also held under the 1852 Act, with surviving material catalogued at the NAI under OL/20. Additional appeals heard under the 1852 Act also exist in this collection for counties Antrim, Cavan, Cork, Donegal, Galway, Kildare, Kilkenny, Leitrim, Mayo, Meath, Monaghan, Sligo, Tipperary, Tyrone and Westmeath, as well as for Dublin City.

A detailed guide to the appeals process, with many fascinating examples, is included in Chapter 6 of Frances McGee's *The Archives of the Valuation of Ireland 1830–1865* (2018, Four Courts Press).

## Valuation Revision Books / Cancelled Land Books

Griffith's initial valuation work was only the start of the process, hence its description as the 'Primary' Valuation of Ireland. Following publication, annual adjustments were then made to the information recorded in subsequent volumes by inspectors who visited properties to note any major changes in their circumstances. In the north these subsequent volumes are referred to today as the Valuation Revision Books, whilst in the south they are called the Cancelled Land Books, although they are the exact same thing.

The individual registers are handwritten and laid out as the information is presented in the Tenement Valuation, with books arranged by poor law union, electoral districts and then townlands. From 1898 onwards, registers for larger cities and county boroughs may be arranged by wards and streets. The books are a goldmine for genealogists and house historians in that they will signify changes in occupancy and ownership, which may indicate that a former holder of a property has sold up, emigrated or passed away.

If a tenant's or lessor's name is cancelled out, it will be scored out with a coloured pencil – look to the far right of the entry on the right-hand page and a year will be written in that same colour, the year of the cancellation. A new owner's name may be added beside the name of the previous tenant or lessor's name. In some entries after 1881 you may see a stamp marked *L.A.P.* beside an entry, which stands for 'Land Act Purchase', and which denotes purchases by tenants of property from their landlords, for which further information may be available from records of the Land Commission (Northern Ireland only at present – p.134), or from the Registry of Deeds or the Land Registry. The phrase 'in fee' beside entries also denotes land held outright by the owner.

PRONI holds over 3,900 revision books for Northern Ireland up to the 1930s, catalogued under VAL/12B, which have now been digitised thanks to a partnership with the Genealogical Society of Utah. Almost 810,000 pages of content provide details of changes of ownership of properties within the six Northern Irish counties, and the county boroughs of Belfast and Londonderry, as well as to the description and value of the holdings. The records can be browsed by townland or parish, but cannot be searched by names of tenants or lessors. For each volume, an index image at the start will provide page numbers for individual townlands, and you can then skip forward or back ten pages at a time, or by a single page at a time.

An equivalent project to digitise the same records for the Republic is currently under way by the Valuation Office (p.9). The institution offers a research service to help trace property history from all of its valuation books.

The following example shows how useful these books were in helping me to finally resolve a twenty-year research brick wall with an ancestor of mine, a three times great-grandmother called Eliza Jane McLaughlin. From her marriage record to William Watton in 1867, Eliza was known to be the daughter of a Thomas McLaughlin, farmer, born in the late 1840s, and at the time of her wedding she was resident at Killowen, by Coleraine, in County Londonderry. The only other possible relative that I knew about was a William McLaughlin, who was recorded as a witness at her wedding. Following their marriage, Eliza and William had briefly lived in Scotland, where they had a child in 1868 who died shortly after birth, after which they returned again to Ireland. In 1868 they then had a daughter Anne, born in the townland of Ballinteer, in the parish of Macosquin, followed by several more children in Ballysally, Coleraine, and in Portstewart. One of these children was my great great-grandfather Cochrane McLaughlin Watton, born in Ballysally townland in 1872.

My problem was that I could not find any connections noted to Eliza Jane in any of the McLaughlin vital records around Coleraine, and there were a few possible Thomas McLaughlins as contenders in the area working as farmers. A theory that she might have come from the townland of Ballinteer, parish of Macosquin, where her first child was born in Ireland, seemed to bear potential fruit when the Valuation Revision Books for the townland noted a Thomas McLaughlin there holding a farm of 26 acres and 15 perches in North Ballinteer until 1887, at which point a change in occupancy was noted with the farm going to the 'Representatives of Thomas McLaughlin', and then in 1889, to a 'Cochrane McLaughlin' – an encouraging development in terms of naming patterns. A death record was found for this Thomas McLaughlin in 1886, confirming the reason for the change of occupancy, but despite all of this sounding very promising, it was still not definitive proof that this was my four times great-grandfather.

It was not until a series of DNA matches was flagged up a few years later that I discovered that I was related to the descendants of another Thomas McLaughlin, born in Ireland in about 1847, who had emigrated to Pennsylvania, USA, before ending his days at Birmingham, Alabama in 1933. This Thomas was quite possibly a candidate for a sibling to Eliza.

In pursuing this new Thomas further, I discovered a newspaper article from *The Allentown Democrat* of 18 September 1901 concerning another gentleman called Cochrane McLaughlin of Catasauqua in Pennsylvania, following his death, which discussed his will going through the probate courts. The article confirmed that Thomas McLaughlin in Alabama was his brother, and gave the names of some additional siblings he had made provision for, including a brother in Ireland, but there was frustratingly still no mention of Eliza Jane. The article did mention, however, that 'the rest and residue of his property, including a leasehold on the old homestead in Ireland, is to be converted into cash, and the proceeds go to his sister in Ireland'.

This now looked promising, and on tracing a copy of the actual will, I finally found the proof I was looking for. After various bequests were listed, including one to his Irish-based brother William McLaughlin, Cochrane had written 'All the remainder and residue of my estate, I will and devise and bequeath unto my sister Mary, now Mary McCloskey, of Ballyntier, County Derry, Ireland'. Just for good measure, he then amended his will with a codicil, and included the line 'I will to my sister Eliza Jane the sum of One Dollar'! A further look at the Valuation Revision Books gratifyingly noted that the farm at North Ballinteer had been transferred by 1904 to a Peter McCloskey, with a further record found in the Registry of Deeds (p.125) showing that the property had been given to him by his wife Mary 'in consideration of the natural love and affection which she the said Mary McCloskey bore towards her husband the said Peter McCloskey'.

This example shows the value of the revision books for research, not just for those based in Ireland, but in many cases for those also based overseas who may still have had property interests in the country that they had left behind.

Following the period covered by these books, researchers will need to consult further records at PRONI from the General Revaluation of Northern Ireland (catalogued under VAL/3), which have their own subsequent revision lists up to 1957. For details of the records for subsequent twentieth-century valuations in Belfast see the PRONI leaflet on Valuation Records (No. 4), accessible from the 'Information Leaflets' section on the home page.

For later valuations in the Republic of Ireland consult the Valuation Office website (p.9).

*Chapter 6*

# TENANCY AND OWNERSHIP

T he greatest body of records noting occupancy of land are those which concern its ownership and tenancies that may have existed. There were many different methods by which land could be owned or rented, and many historic grievances over who could take possession of particular properties.

Most people in Ireland held and rented land by way of a lease from large estate owners, but there were several ways to do so, which conveyed different rights to the tenants affected.

In this chapter I will examine some of the records specifically concerning the ownership of the land and its value.

### Estate records
Some of the most useful records that can be used to trace our ancestors' presence in a particular area are those of the large estate owners. The records can tell us about the development of their estates across time, and also the amount of land owned by the landed gentry, and how it was managed. In addition to original land grants from landholders, letter books, petitions and accounts, records such as copies of leases, lease books and rentals concerning the tenants can also be particularly helpful – not only in determining the land ownership pattern in a given area at any one time, and its value, but also in identifying ancestors and relatives, particularly when the vital records have failed to survive.

Across much of Ireland, a real scourge was the absenteeism of landlords, many of whom were of the landed gentry resident in Britain, whilst across much of the country many of the great estate owners who were present failed to invest any expense or effort into relationships with their tenantry. In rural Ireland in particular, many tenants were treated as a source of income only, with little to no security of tenure offered. The failure of many estate holders to implement reforms and to adapt to changing circumstances can offer additional resources to help us trace the fortunes of our ancestors, particularly after the Famine, not just with the records documenting bankruptcies of estates but through the redistribution of land and democratisation of ownership more universally as a consequence.

The two key questions concerning estate records are: a) who was the estate owner? and b) have the relevant records survived? There are many possible ways to try to determine who a likely estate owner was. In some records, such as the 1901 and 1911 censuses (p.54), and the records for Griffith's Valuation and subsequent revisions (p.97), the name of the landlord is given. He or she may have been the estate owner or perhaps a 'middleman', leasing land from the estate owner and then subletting it for an increased rent (p.104). If it was the latter then there will also be an entry for that person noting from whom their property was held. Newspapers are a further useful resource, particularly for advertisements concerning sales in a particular townland or region (p.75), and of course, contemporary directories (p.69) and gazetteers (p.146) will also provide the names of the landed gentry for the area.

A particular problem with locating surviving estate records is that they can be held in a variety of repositories, or still be held by the

*Kildalton College in Piltown, Co. Kilkenny, was previously an estate owned by the Earls of Bessborough.*

families themselves. There are, however, several guides available online that can help.

For the province of Ulster, PRONI has an online guide, 'Family tree – landed estate records', at **www.nidirect.gov.uk/publications/family-tree-landed-estate-records**, as well as a guide to 'Significant privately deposited archives' at **www.nidirect.gov.uk/articles/significant-privately-deposited-archives**. In addition, PRONI is also a contributor to the Irish Archive Resources platform at **www.iar.ie**, where several collections have been catalogued that include material for landowners who held property north and south of the modern border. Appendix 2 of William Roulston's *Researching Scots-Irish Ancestors (2nd edition)* carries a detailed description of estate records for the seventeenth and eighteenth centuries for some 350 estates in Ulster, arranged county by county, and by the surnames or seat names of the estate holders. John Grenham's *Tracing Your Irish Ancestors* details some additional estate records holdings on an all-island basis in his County Source Lists chapter.

In the Republic, the National Archives of Ireland has a 'Guide to family and landed estate collections' available at **www.nationalarchives.ie/genealogy1/genealogy-records/private-source-records**, whilst the NLI provides advice in its manuscripts section at **www.nli.ie/en/collections-manuscripts-introduction.aspx** on 'Landed Estate Papers and Deeds' and 'Irish Landed Estates, Rentals and Maps'. Many of the facility's holdings are searchable using its 'Catalogue and Sources' databases. Information concerning the ownership of estates within the provinces of Connacht and Munster is also available on the University of Galway's Landed Estates Database at **www.landedestates.ie** for the period from 1700 to 1914.

It is also possible that records may not be held in Ireland at all. A typical example is the Hasting (Irish) Papers, as held in the Huntington Library, California, USA, which provide a great deal of material on the practices of estate management in the Lagan Valley in Ulster by the Conway and Rawdon families. The collection is described in some detail by Brenda Collins in *Familia: Ulster Genealogical Review*, Number 24, 2008.

## Freeholders

In Ireland, the term 'freeholder' was given to those who owned their land outright, or tenants who held land through a lease lasting a lifetime, or for more than one life (p.107).

Originally, a freeholder was a person who owned their land outright by holding what was known as the 'fee simple' to their particular property, or who held it on the basis of 'fee tail', an arrangement which permitted the conveyance of the property through inheritance only to direct lines of the original granter, and in its entirety. Such an arrangement was adopted by many to essentially preserve the wealth and power of a family in an area; however, land that was so *entailed* in this way eventually became a real problem for the landed gentry in the aftermath of the Famine. Many found themselves in debt due to the many financial burdens they had which could not be resolved by simply flogging off parts of their estates, one of the many factors which led to the creation of the Encumbered Estates Courts (p.113).

A form of tenure that was used commonly during the Plantation of Ulster and in subsequent urban settlements across the country was land that was held through what was termed a 'fee farm' grant, in which a property was conveyed to a purchaser for a large up-front payment to an estate owner (who held the original fee simple). In this arrangement, although the property on a holding was owned by the purchaser and could be considered a freehold property, the land itself was still subject to an annual ground rent payment to the original owner. Historically, such ground rents were not subject to inflation, meaning that over time many became minimal, to the point where they became 'nominal'.

In both Northern Ireland and the Republic of Ireland there are schemes to permit holders of fee farm land and leaseholders to buy out their ground rent obligations, and to convert their properties into freeholds.

*Freeholders' records from the province of Ulster can be viewed on the PRONI website.*

## Leases

The most common form of landholding in Ireland was by leasehold, of which there were several forms.

Landlords could grant tenants set leases for their holdings, with both parties retaining a copy of the agreement, the counterpart going to the tenant. In such an arrangement the landlord is styled as the 'lessor', and the tenant as the 'lessee'. In return for the use of the land a rent would be charged, payable usually twice a year to the landlord on what were known as 'gale days', usually in the spring and autumn on the quarter days of 1 May and 1 November. Prior to the nineteenth century, it was common for rent to be delivered through a mixture of monetary payment and in kind, through agricultural yield, and/or through some form of labour or service.

The main form of leasehold involved agreements regarding tenancy for a set number of years, often for a traditional twenty-one-, or thirty-one-year period, but the length of a lease could be for much longer, to the order of several hundred years. One of the most famous examples of such an arrangement was the signing of a 9,000-year lease of 4 acres of land in Dublin by Arthur Guinness on 31 December 1759, with an annual rent due of £45. The site has since been purchased outright. A lease could also be set at the whim of the landlord through a 'tenancy at will', an agreement which could be terminated by either party at any stage.

Tenants with lengthy leases over large holdings could, if permitted by their landlord, sublet parts of their holdings to 'undertenants', and assume the role of a middleman. In areas where estate owners were absent, the middlemen could become quite important figures within the community.

During the period of the Penal Laws there were many restrictions on the ownership of land by Roman Catholics. The Act to Prevent the Further Growth of Popery in 1704 (p.118) led to Catholics being denied the right to inherit land from Protestants, and to buy land. The Catholic Relief Act of 1774 continued the ban, but did allow Catholics to acquire leases of up to 999 years, without any of the political rights held by freeholders (p.102).

Nevertheless, one of the major grievances in much of Ireland prior to the Famine was the insecurity of tenure on many leases held, in contrast to the practice of 'tenant right' established in the north after the Plantations, also known as the Ulster Custom. This permitted tenants a right of renewal for leases without sudden escalations in the rate of rent demanded upon renewal or termination, but also compensation for any improvements made to a holding during the period of a tenancy.

Although an attempt was made to address this issue in the British Parliament in 1845, following the establishment of the Commission on Occupation of Land (Ireland) two years earlier, better known as the 'Devon Commission', it would not be until 1881 that the Ulster Custom practice was eventually extended across the whole of Ireland. Many interviews with leaseholders gathered by the Devon Commission can be read within the House of Commons Parliamentary Papers (p.74).

Leases can be incredibly useful documents for research. A typical example from 1824 was a lease granted by Arthur Lord Viscount Dungannon to my four times great-grandfather, John Montgomery, for a small holding in the townland of Drumgurland, within the County Antrim parish of Islandmagee. The introduction on the lease conveys the date of the agreement, the parties to the agreement, and the land in question:

> This Indenture made the twenty second Day of december [*sic*] in the Year of Our Lord One Thousand Eight Hundred and twenty four BETWEEN the Honorable [*sic*] ARTHUR LORD VISCOUNT DUNGANNON of the one part and John Montgomery of the Townland of drumgurland [*sic*] in the parish of Island Magee and County of Antrim Farmer WITNESSETH, that the said LORD VISCOUNT DUNGANNON hath demised, granted, released and confirmed, and by these Presents doth demise, grant, release and confirm, unto the said John Montgomery All that farm and lands in his actual possession now being, by virtue of a bargain and sale to him and them thereof made by the said VISCOUNT, by Indenture bearing date the day next before the day of the date of these Presents for one whole Year from thence next ensuing, in consideration of Five Shillings sterling, and by force of the Statute for transferring Uses into Possession, ALL THAT AND THOSE, the Farm, Tenement, and Parcel of Land, contained by Survey One acre three roods and twenty seven perches plantation measure or thereabouts be the same more or less and now in the actual possession or occupation of the said John Montgomery his undertenants or assigns…

This established the amount to be leased, and noted it to be reckoned in plantation measure (p.43). There then followed a lengthy description of some of the rights to the land that the viscount retained, such as the right to minerals, timber, moss, as well as rights of way to other parts of his lands.

The next crucial part is a section outlining the duration of the lease, and any rents and fees to be paid, as well as their due dates:

TO HAVE AND TO HOLD all the singular said Premises, with their Rights, members and Appurtenances (except as before excepted) unto the said John Montgomery and his and their Heirs, Executors, Administrators and Assigns, for and during the full end term and time of Thirty one years commencing from the first of November, One Thousand Eight Hundred and twenty three from thenceforth fully to be complete and ended: He the said John Montgomery his Heirs, Executors, Administrators and Assigns, YIELDING AND PAYING therefore and thereout, Yearly and every Year during this Demise, unto the said VISCOUNT, his Heirs and Assigns, the clear yearly Rent or Sum of Two pounds seventeen shillings and six pence sterling, together with One Shilling for each Pound of Rent, as Agent's Fees, and One Shilling Yearly for Acquittances, and Two Days work for a Man and a Horse yearly, if required, or Three Shillings Sterling in lieu thereof as Duties at the Election of the said VISCOUNT, his Heirs and Assigns, over and above all Taxes, Subsidies and Impositions whatsoever, imposed or to be imposed (Quit, Crown, and Chief Rents, only excepted). The said yearly Rent and Fees to be paid Half-yearly, by two equal Portions, on every first day of May, and every first day of November, yearly, and during this Demise.

In addition to the payment of money, John, as the viscount's tenant, also had to undertake to fulfil certain other conditions. He had to agree to grind any corn or grain at the mill of Islandmagee, upon penalty of 5 shillings for every barrel found to have been ground at any other mill, and he had to agree to be legally summoned to carry out jury service at the court leet and court baron of the manor of Castle Chichester (p.41). After then essentially agreeing to look after his property, the lease was duly signed at the end by the landlord and his tenant, with wax seals beside each name, as well as the signature of a witness.

When consulting these leases, I found several granted on the same date to a few other family members in the parish, but of particular note was one granted to John's kinsman Hugh Montgomery. Whereas John had taken on a lease for 1 acre, 3 roods and 27 perches, Hugh took on a much larger holding in the same townland of Drumgurland, at 14 acres, 1 rood and 29 perches. In trying to establish why John's holding was so small, I later discovered a vital clue from a published parish history.

At the end of the eighteenth century, the inhabitants of Islandmagee were mainly descended from Scottish Presbyterian immigrants who had settled there at the start of the previous century. In 1798, when the United Irishmen had arisen in rebellion, the men of Islandmagee had all turned out to support the uprising. The parish history notes how John was to receive a lifelong disability as a consequence:

> The subject of this notice was fifteen years of age at the time of the turn-out in '98, and as a result of a boyish prank with a loaded weapon which had fallen into his hands an accident deprived him of several fingers, thereby making him partially unfit for manual labour. His parents consequently gave him every opportunity within their means of acquiring a knowledge of those subjects which might prove useful to him as a teacher, and which he afterwards taught with singular success.

Due to his disability, John was incapable of making a living as a farmer. Instead, he grew up to work as a teacher in Islandmagee, and for a time, also served as a justice of the peace.

An alternative type of agreement which appeared from the late seventeenth century onwards was that known as a 'lease for lives', which was heritable. Theoretically this could act as a lease in perpetuity, with the holder of such a document considered to be a freeholder, even though a token rent was still due to the original landlord in question. In such a lease, land was granted initially for the duration of the lives of three individuals, and remained current so long as those named were alive. However, when one of those named in the document passed away, it was possible to have the lease renewed with the inclusion of a new third name, upon payment of a 'renewal fine'. This system can be particularly useful for researchers because the continual renewal of the arrangement often led to considerably more documentation between the lessor and the lessees.

The following is a good eighteenth-century example of such a practice from the town of Larne in County Antrim, concerning another branch of my Montgomery family.

An initial lease by the Earl of Antrim was granted to Hugh Montgomery (noted as 'Montgomrey' in the document), merchant of Larne, on 1 September 1743, for the following piece of land:

> ...the Tenement situate on the south side of the main street of Larne bounded on the west end by William Montgomreys Tenement on

the east end by James Boyds Tenement Containing in front fourty [*sic*] foot and backwards to the foot of the Garden...

The document itself is a packed statement detailing all rights and privileges concerning the land, written in some fairly extraordinary legal language that can easily sap the soul, but the key part, in addition to its date and the identification of the location, is the duration for the lease, given in terms of the lives of two other individuals in addition to Hugh:

TO HAVE AND TO HOLD all and singular the said demised Premises, with their and every of their Rights, members, Appendances and Appurtenances, (except before excepted) unto the said Hugh Montgomrey his Heirs and Assigns, for and during the natural Life and Lives of the afforesaid Hugh Montgomrey the Leasee and for and During the natural life of Widow Karr of Larne aged eighty five years or thereabouts and for and Dureing [*sic*] the natural life of Robert Montgomery brother to the Leasee aged Sixteen years or thereabouts...

Quite how Hugh Montgomery was related to 'Widow Karr' (Kerr), if indeed he was, is unknown, but the document provides some exceptionally useful genealogical detail. In addition to naming a 16-year-old brother, Robert, it also names a next-door neighbour, William Montgomery, who may well have been a further relative.

However, the lease, when called up at PRONI, was also found to have three further smaller documents appended to its front by a piece of string. These noted updates to the original agreement in subsequent years. The first occurred in 1756, and is worth outlining in full:

TO ALL PEOPLE, to whom these Presents shall come: KNOW YE, That I, the Right Honourable Alexander Earl of Antrim, at the Instance and Request of Hugh Montgomery and upon Payment of the Sum of Thirteen Shillings and Fourpence Sterl. as a fine received by me for the Fall of one of the Lives within mentioned, to witt, Widow Keer [Kerr] the receipt whereof I do hereby acknowledge, and thereof do acquit and discharge the said Hugh Montgomery, and at his Desire and Request, and upon the Nomination of another Life in place and stead of one so failing as aforesaid, I the said Alexander Earl of Antrim do by these Presents, for me, my heirs and Assigns, according to the Purport and true Meaning of the within Demise, add and insert the Life of Robt Agnew, Youngest son to James Agnew of Larne merchant in the room and place of the said Widow Keer TO HAVE AND TO HOLD all and singular the Premises within demised, with the Appurtenances, unto the said Hugh Montgomery, his heirs and Assigns, for and during the natural Life and Lives of the said Hugh Montgomery, Robert Montgomery, brother to said Hugh, and Robt Agnew, Youngest Son to James Agnew of Larne, Merchant, and the Survivors and Survivor of them; at and under the yearly Rent, Receiver's Fees, Duties, Covenants, Reservations, Provisoes, Conditions and Agreements in the within Lease mentioned and contained. IN WITNESS whereof the said Alexander Earl of Antrim, and the said Hugh Montgomery have hereunto set their hands and Seals, this first Day of November one thousand, seven hundred and Fifty Six.

In this example, Hugh had deliberately nominated the youngest son of James Agnew to act as the new third name, to extend the duration of the lease for as long as possible.

The next renewal found appended to the original lease is dated to 8 July 1776. In this, the pre-printed wording is almost identical, save that Alexander Earl of Antrim has since been succeeded by Randal-William, Earl of Antrim. In this document, Hugh Montgomery was himself now removed from the list of names, at the request of his son and heir Samuel Montgomery, indicating that Hugh had since passed away. Replacing Hugh as the new third name was 'his Royal Highness George Prince of Wales'. This became a very common practice on leases from the end of the eighteenth century onwards, as it would be assumed that the heir to the throne would have a considerable life ahead of him! This particular Prince George was in fact the future King George III (1760–1820). The lease was now therefore valid for the lifetimes of Samuel Montgomery, Robert Agnew, and Prince George. For an explanation as to why there was not another document before this showing a substitution of Hugh for Samuel, see p.120.

The final attachment to the lease was a further renewal and update from 20 February 1786, made at the request of Martha Montgomery, 'the Widow & relic of Hugh Montgomery late of Larne in ye County of Antrim Gent[lema]n deceas[e]d'. In this document, Robert Agnew is noted as having passed on, and in his place a new name was added, being Hugh Casement, son of George Casement of Larne in the County of Antrim, Gentleman, aged just 3 years. The lease was now in Martha's name for the duration of the lives of Samuel Montgomery, His Royal Highness George Augustus Prince of Wales and the said Hugh Casement.

The need to continually renew the lease for lives became something of a bureaucratic nightmare. Following the Renewable Leaseholds Conversion Act of 1849, any leases for lives granted from 1 August 1849 onwards were instead treated as if they were fee farm grants (p.103), whilst those already holding leases for lives could convert their leases into fee farm grants.

## Rental records

In addition to leases, a further type of record connecting landlords to their tenants was that of the rents due and paid. Surviving rental records can help to trace the occupancy of a piece of land, the size of the land held, and the money due for it, with such payments paid annually or twice yearly on term days. The records can also identify if there were any arrears due in payments, and any transfers of occupancy.

In some parts of the country, there was a custom of tenants being granted a six-month period of grace upon taking on a new holding, placing them into arrears from the gale day (p.104) on which their rent would be due, following the harvest of crops, in a practice known as the 'hanging gale'. Upon any default their cattle could be impounded and they could be evicted.

Where rental records exist, they might provide a chronological run for several years, indeed decades, detailing occupancy, but there is also a downside, in that not all of the tenants in an area may be listed. The landlord was primarily concerned with his income, and in cases where land may have been leased to a tenant, and then further subdivided again by him into smaller lets to his own undertenants, it may only be the payments from the landlord's immediate tenants or middlemen (p.104) that are noted in his account books. In such cases, however, estate correspondence may still refer to some of the undertenants. Nevertheless, a good set of records will often reveal a great deal of information, but they may also introduce new questions about your family's presence in a particular area.

In the previous section, I showed that my four times great-grandfather John Montgomery had taken on a lease in 1824 in the townland of Drumgurland, parish of Islandmagee, from Arthur Lord Viscount Dungannon, as had his kinsman Hugh Montgomery. The surviving rental book for the area, which commenced in 1818 and continued until 1858, in fact reveals quite a bit more about Hugh's situation. Although Hugh did sign a lease in 1824, the rental book notes that he was already a tenant in the townland of Drumgurland in 1818. The first entry for him was noted as follows:

Drumgurland
Hugh Montgomery

| | |
|---|---|
| Arrears due 1st November 1818 | £---------- |
| Half a year's rent due 1st May 1819 | £3 15s 9d |
| Half a year's rent due 1st Nov 1819 | £3 15s 9d |
| Cash received | £3 15s 9d |
| Arrears due 1st Nov 1819 | £3 15s 9d |

(Source: Rentals 1818 Lord Viscount Dungannon Island Magee D1954/1/1)

In 1824, when the new lease was granted to Hugh, the amount he had to pay to his landlord had doubled:

Drumgurland
Hugh Montgomery

| | |
|---|---|
| Arrears due 1 NOV 1824 | ---------- |
| Half a year's due MAY 1825 | £7 10s |
| Half a year's due NOV 1825 | £7 10s |
| Received | £7 10s |
| Received | £7 10s |
| Arrears due NOV 1825 | ---------- |

At this point, John's first entry appears in the rental book:

Drumgurland
John Montgomery

| | |
|---|---|
| Arrears due 1 NOV 1824 | £1 10s |
| Half a year's due MAY 1825 | £1 10s |
| Half a year's due NOV 1825 | £1 10s |
| Received | £3 |
| Received | ---------- |
| Arrears due NOV 1825 | ---------- |

Both Montgomery gentlemen (who were likely brothers) continued to reside at Drumgurland, but by the 1840s, John's circumstances changed. At some stage in the mid-1840s John sold up his tenancy at Drumgurland, and relocated to a larger plot of land in the adjacent townland of Dundressan, which he worked in partnership with a gentleman by the name of Davidson, as noted in this entry from 1848:

Dundressan
Davison & Montgomery

| | | |
|---|---|---|
| Arrears at Nov 1847 | £7 | 1s 2d |
| ½ year due May 1848 | £9 | 19s 10d |
| ½ year due Nov 1848 | £9 | 19s 10d |
| Recd | £19 14s 8d | |
| Poor rate allowed | 5s | |

The payments continued as such until 1858, the last recorded year in the rental book. Although only his surname is shown at Dundressan, I know this was definitely a record for my ancestor, for the simple reason that John noted the details of the land purchase with James Davidson in a school log book which he also used as a jotter, in an undated entry recorded between two other entries on the same page, dated to 1842 and 1850. In this record he tallies the amounts of land that he owns, in acres, roods and perches (p.43):

First I bought from Alexander Barr 3A 2R 0P
Secondly I bought from John Stewart 4A 2R 27P
Also I hold the half of 42 Ps & Jas Davidson the other 21Ps
All the land that I Jn Montgomery hold is 8A 1R 18P
Also James Davidson holds 4A 0R 36 P
All the land added together Amts to 12A 2R 14P

A further note in John's log book from 1860 comments again on his land holdings, showing that he had further expanded them:

Islandmagee July 19th 1860 This day Mr Murdough
Told me the number of acres I hold under him
Fifteen acres two roods & thirty eight perches 14A 2R 38P

A year later John's holdings were found recorded in Griffith's Valuation, and in subsequent years in the Valuation Revision Books (p.97).

Whilst most rentals will have to be dug out from an archival repository somewhere, some have been digitised and made available online. By far the most significant collection is the Landed Estates Court Rentals collection from the National Archives of Ireland.

Following the Famine, many landowners had suffered a loss of income from tenants and devaluation of their land, forcing many towards bankruptcy. Many were trapped within their own aristocratic establishments, unable to sell their estates due to them being

*Montgomery family graves at Ballypriormore, Islandmagee, County Antrim.*

'encumbered' with obligations to pay set amounts to family members as part of marriage settlements, and previous provisions as set out in wills and entails prior to its inheritance.

The Encumbered Estates Acts of 1848 and 1849 allowed landowners to free themselves from these burdens, by selling their estates to the state, which could then redistribute them to new owners with a new title granted, clear of any previous burdens or debts. The Encumbered Estates Court set up in 1849 was replaced by Landed Estates Courts three years later, and then from 1872 by a Land Judges Court to further ease the process. As part of the sales processes, catalogues were drawn up for each estate, which included details of the rentals of properties present with them.

The Landed Estate Court rentals can be consulted on microfilm at the NAI, catalogued under MFGS/39/1-66, whilst a copy of the eighty-two bound volumes for the whole of Ireland is equally available at PRONI in Belfast, catalogued under D/1201 (with an index on microfilm at MIC80/2). The records are also available online in Findmypast's 'Landed Estates Court Rentals 1850–1885' collection, which includes copies of maps for the estates in question, where available. Some further rentals from the post-1885 period, as held by the Quit Rent Office (p.115), are available for consultation at the NAI.

A good example from the collection, showing the amount of detail that can be returned, concerns a sale of lands in 1859 belonging to an Arthur O'Beirne, noted as a minor, as enabled by his guardian, Mary O'Beirne, administratrix and widow of the deceased and intestate John Lewis Mullaniffe O'Beirne. Five lots were put up for sale at midday on Thursday, 24 November 1859 in the Landed Estates Court at 14 Henrietta Street, Dublin.

If we take a look at the second lot, the details are presented in a table, which notes that it is for part of the lands of Trillick or Trillickacurry, within the barony of Moydow in County Longford, and as being 'Held in Fee', i.e. owned outright by O'Beirne. His tenants are noted as the Representatives of Charles Twaddle, and the extent of the land concerned stated as 20A Irish measure, or 32A 1R 23P English measure (i.e. statute measure), with an annual rental value of £18 9s 2½d, and the gale days for rent due given as 25 March and 29 September. Under the 'Date and Description of Instrument' column we then get the following:

Lease dated the 26th January, 1795, made by James Mullaniffe to Charles Twaddle, of All That and Those, that part of the lands of Trillickacurry, containing, by a survey, 20 acres, or thereabouts, plantation measure more or less, together with the bog thereunto belonging. To hold from the 25th day of March last past, for the term of 999 years, or for ever, at the yearly rent of £20 late Irish currency above taxes.

With the basics defined on the tenure, further conditions with the lease are described in the 'Observations' column, which also notes the names of the deceased tenant's representatives:

This lease contains the usual powers of distress and entry on non-payment of rent, and covenants between landlord and tenant; and there is also a covenant by the lessee for him, his heirs, and assigns, not to sell, assign, alien, or transfer, or make over to any person any part of said premises without the consent in writing of the lessors, under hand and seal, but that all said premises, with the appurtenances, should revert to Mary Mulloy, otherwise Twaddle, and to her children by the said Charles Twaddle.

A counterpart of this lease will be handed to the purchaser.

The rent of this holding is paid by Robert Twaddle and Charles Twaddle, representatives of original lessee, in equal moieties.

The second part of the page then has a section entitled 'Tenure of Lands and Conditions of Sale'. This can often contain a great deal of background history of a property ownership, but in this case it merely confirms again that the lot is held in fee, followed by a disclaimer to the accuracy of the description of the stated lot.

Findmypast also hosts a database of records created in 1907 by the Estates Commissioners Office, which lists people who had submitted applications as an evicted tenant, or as a representative on an evicted tenant's behalf, in pursuit of relief after the eviction.

Additional information from rental rolls for northern estates can be found at **www.ancestryireland.com/search-irish-genealogy-databases**, whilst some rental rolls and estate records from counties Antrim, Armagh, Carlow, Cavan, Clare, Donegal, Down, Galway, Kilkenny and Londonderry are available within the 'Genealogy' section of the From Ireland website (**www.from-ireland.net**).

## Estate maps

Within estate papers collections you may also be lucky to find contemporary maps of the areas for which the rentals were concerned or for where leases were granted. For the previously noted rentals found for my Montgomery family in Islandmagee (p.110) I was also lucky to find two maps at PRONI. The first, from 1841 and catalogued under D3313/1A, depicted the townlands on Con McNeill's lands at a scale of 16 perches to the inch (p.43), but the second, catalogued under D1954/6/68 and dating to c.1850, was much more specific for the townland of Kilcoan to the west of the peninsula. At a scale of 4 chains to the inch, it showed each property and the surnames of the families in residence alongside them, and on the fields which they farmed.

In addition to the main national archives north and south, the Linen Hall Library in Belfast has many estate maps in its collection, as has the NLI in Dublin. The National Archives of Ireland also hosts many maps in its estates collections, as detailed in its online guide at **www.nationalarchives.ie/article/guide-landed-estate-records**.

## The Quit Rent Office

A 'Quit Rent' was a hangover from the Books of Survey and Distribution from Cromwellian times (p.22), which was paid until the 1930s. It was essentially a small sum paid by freeholders on manors in the redistributed lands granted to them in the seventeenth century following the confiscations of land from Roman Catholics, which freed them of any feudal obligations to the Crown. Over time, the value of the Quit Rent diminished so much that it became a token payment.

The revenue due was collected by the Quit Rent Office in Dublin, which also oversaw the management of Crown estates in Ireland, such as Phoenix Park and the Curragh in Kildare. The office's work was eventually transferred to the Irish Land Commission (p.131) in the Republic in 1943, with its records, which include rentals, leases and other materials, now held at the NAI, catalogued under QRO/1-9, and QRO/DS (for the Down Survey).

For more on the collections held visit **www.archivesportaleurope.net/ ead-display/-/ead/pl/aicode/IE-NAI/type/fa/id/QRO**.

## Manor records

During the Plantations of the seventeenth century, the manorial system (p.41) was revived as a means to help administer estates in Ireland, with the re-establishment of manorial courts. Although not many records have survived for the majority of the country, in the areas where they do they can be particularly useful for research. A parliamentary enquiry in 1837 noted the existence at that stage of some 204 such courts in Ireland, with over half in Ulster and a quarter in Munster, although by now most were acting almost exclusively in the capacity of small debts courts. Manorial courts were formally abolished in Ireland in 1857, after the introduction of Crown Courts across the country.

In 1604, the Earl of Antrim, Randal MacDonnell, was granted a charter to hold manorial courts on his lands, and duly established four in the four lower baronies of his estates in the north of Antrim, which were located in his manors at Ballycastle, Dunluce, Glenarm and Oldstone. The court leet (also termed 'a view of frankpledge') was originally a criminal court comprising a jury of freeholders which heard petty common law offences, but its role was soon taken over by the role of magistrates, leaving it with purely administrative functions. The court baron handled civil cases, such as cases involving debts, with its work later subsumed into a new 'court of record', established from 1629, which could hear claims up to the value of £10. In charge of the courts was an appointed judicial officer known as a *seneschal*.

The earlier responsibilities of these courts also included the registration of deeds and leases, although the nature of cases later heard became more petty, as a civil court structure began to emerge in the counties. The earliest surviving records from the courts date to 1742, and are held at PRONI under D/2977. An article by Ian Montgomery in the Ulster Historical Foundation's *Familia* publication from 2000 (Number 16) gives a comprehensive overview of the areas that they covered.

'The Manor Courts of the Earl of Thomond 1666–1686' by S. C. O'Mahony, published in 2004 within *Analecta Hibernica* (2004, No. 38, p.135, 137–220), provides a detailed overview of the work in the Earl of Thomond's estates within County Clare. In the work of the courts, O'Mahony notes that 'All of society is there: Esquires, gentlemen, merchants, tradesmen, farmers, labourers, with Gael and Gall at every level.' The source for the material published is found in a manuscript within the Petworth Papers of the Earls of Egremont, as held at West Sussex Record Office in Chichester, England (catalogued as Ms C 10/7), and again showcasing that not all records concerning Ireland may necessarily be found in Ireland. It includes material for the West Clare manors of Crovraghan, Kilrush, Moigh, Finavarra, Innish and Clonrond, Bunratty, Doonass and Castlebank, as well as for Fedamore in County Limerick and Cullen in County Tipperary.

The following is a typical example of information from Killadysert that might be found for a tenancy, in this case as presented to 'the Court Leet and Court baron for the manor of Cruovraghan at Killodeesert' on 15 October 1672:

We further present that we cannot find Bryen Swyny to be tenant to the half plowland of Moyeh, that it is Teige o Lemessy who now produced his lease thereof from Thomas Hickman Esq., the said earl's steward, being for 21 years commencing the 25th day of

*The manor house at Ormond Castle, by Carrick-on-Suir, Co. Tipperary, built in the 1560s by Thomas Butler, 10th Earl of Ormonde. It is the best preserved example of a Tudor manor house in Ireland.*

March 1666, set for £8 sterling per annum, together with 8s and 9d duties within 7 years to build a house of 8 couples with stone wall, stone chimneys, plastered and ruffcasted within the time of seven years, to plant an orchard of 30 apple and pear trees, not to alien, to pay a heriott, to leave all improvements in good repair. We find the house built without stone wall or stone chimneys, the orchard planted.

O'Mahony's article can be accessed through subscription access via JSTOR (**www.jstor.org**).

Elsewhere, Raymond Gillespie's article 'A Manor Court in Seventeenth Century Ireland' in *Irish Economic and Social History* (1998, Vol. 25, pp.81–7) cites many further examples of the work of manorial courts in Limerick, Dublin, Cork and Counties Antrim, Armagh, Clare and Kilkenny.

## Inheritance laws

Prior to the seventeenth century, the law of 'gavelkind' was widely used across Gaelic Ireland to pass on land to heirs. This law essentially led to the division of the deceased's lands to all of his sons, including any who were illegitimate. Its application varied across the country; on some estates the land was divided equally, on others the best portion was reserved to the lord, or land could be divided up according to age and status. In 1606, an Act of the Irish Parliament formally abolished gavelkind and instead imposed the law of primogeniture, as practised in England, with the eldest son inheriting all of the deceased's heritable property.

This was later reversed in 1704, when the Act to Prevent the Further Growth of Popery imposed gavelkind once again on Roman Catholics as the form of inheritance if the eldest son refused to conform to the Anglican religion – in other words, if he refused to become a Protestant he would lose out on most of his inheritance by the law of primogeniture, and receive only a part share alongside his brothers. The inheritance of land from Protestants by Catholics was also forbidden by the Act, as was the right for Catholics to buy land or to take on leases longer than thirty-one years.

Within a few decades, the result of this Act was to drastically reduce the amount of land held by Catholics. As sectarian attitudes began to thaw later in the eighteenth century, the Catholic Relief Act of 1778 allowed Catholics to bequeath land to a single heir through primogeniture if they had first sworn an oath of allegiance to the Crown.

## Probate records

Probate records are some of the most important documents concerning the ownership of property. If a will was left it could outline the intended heir or heirs to the deceased's property, including any heritable estate, or in the event of no will being left, how the deceased's estate was to be disposed of by a court-appointed executor or executors. The court-based probate process was originally handled by the Church of Ireland, but following the implementation of the Probates and Letters of Administration Act (Ireland) 1857, it became a process of the civil courts from 1858 onwards. This continues to be the case to this day in both the Republic of Ireland and Northern Ireland.

The ecclesiastical courts of the Church of Ireland involved were called the 'consistorial' courts (also known as diocesan courts) and the 'prerogative' court. A consistorial court held jurisdiction over a single Anglican diocese (p.40) within which the deceased's estate was based. The Prerogative Court of the Archbishop of Armagh was the superior court, and handled probate cases where property was held in more than one diocese, and at a value of over £5 at least within each.

If the deceased died 'testate', i.e. left a will, then once the document was presented to the court a grant of probate would be issued, authenticating the will and conveying the responsibility to dispose of the estate to the executor or executors nominated by the deceased. If the deceased died 'intestate', however, and no will was left, then if presented to the court for disposal, the court would appoint an administrator for the estate, normally a member of the family or a creditor seeking the repayment of debts owed. The administrator would be required to take out an administrative bond with sureties, to guarantee that his or her responsibilities were carried out honestly and effectively to draw up an inventory of the deceased's estate. Once presented to the court, a letter of administration (also known as an 'admon') would be granted, allowing the administrator to act as the executor to dispose of the estate.

Grants of probate tend to be the more fruitful of the court-based documents, often containing a great deal of genealogical information, but even admons can have some use, if the administrator was a family member. Not all cases made it to the courts, however, as families were often able to handle the conveyance of smaller estates between themselves.

Earlier in this chapter I discussed the leases for lives for property held by the Montgomery family in Larne, County Antrim (p.107). A lease for lives granted in 1743 to Hugh Montgomery, in his name and for the lives of himself, his brother Robert and a Widow Karr, was later renewed in 1756 upon the death of Widow Karr, with her name substituted for that of a young lad called Robert Agnew. In 1776 the lease was again renewed, but Hugh was himself no longer mentioned within it, with the person asking for the renewal instead being his son Samuel. There was no document within the bundle that recorded a substitution for Hugh's name with that of Samuel. The property was in fact inherited by Samuel from his father, with the inheritance specified in a will and recorded with a grant of probate.

In comparison to the lease, the will was considerably more detailed with regards not only to the genealogical information contained, but also some description of the properties in question. In it, Hugh Montgomery, a merchant in Larne, started by bequeathing

> …unto my son Samuel Montgomery of Larne aforesaid Merchant both my Freeholds or Freehold Interests in the town of Larne aforesaid and all personal fortune of every kind soever…

He then empowered Samuel to make legacy and annuity provisions for his wife and daughters, by empowering him to raise a mortgage bond against the value of this freehold estate. The will then notes that his wife, Martha Montgomery or Brown, was to receive an annual annuity of £25 sterling, to be made in half-yearly payments. If this payment was not made, Martha was then empowered to take possession of the property herself to sell off what she needed to in order to realise the funds for the annuity.

Hugh further granted Martha all of the household furniture, asking her to dispose of this herself by a further will or deed in her lifetime to their son Samuel and to their two daughters. The house where Hugh was in residence when writing the will was also to go to Martha until such time as his son married, and he describes the property as having offices and gardens. If Samuel was indeed to marry, then he was to 'fit up in a genteel manner the House wherein Mr Riddle now Dwells', also noted to contain offices and gardens.

Descriptions of legacies to be paid to his daughters Margaret and Martha follow, and a further note made that if Samuel died without issue, then Hugh's two properties were to go to his two daughters. If one died before the other, the surviving daughter was to receive the full share of the estate.

Hugh made a further provision, should neither of his children bear any children of their own. In this case, his freeholds were to go to his 'kinsman' William Montgomery, merchant of Larne, and if he failed to have children, then to William's brother John Montgomery of Larne. Just for good measure, Hugh adds that both were the sons of John Montgomery, merchant of Larne, who was asked to oversee Martha's handling of the estate as Hugh's sole executrix. The probate for the will was granted on 10 October 1778 to Martha.

I was extremely lucky to locate a copy of this will, for the church court documents recording probate cases prior to 1858 have unfortunately largely been destroyed as a consequence of the Civil War. In fact, the detail I have just quoted from Hugh Montgomery's will does not come from the original document at all, but a later typed copy that was created prior to the original's destruction in Dublin.

Although most of the pre-1858 will and grants books have been tragically destroyed, many copies of individual documents were made across the country for a variety of reasons, and a great deal of effort has since been put into retrieving as many of these as possible. Other sources such as Inland Revenue registers also contain some pre-1858 abstracts.

### Finding pre-1858 probate records

The NAI hosts a 'Guide to testamentary records' at **www.nationalarchives. ie/article/testamentary-record**, and amongst its digitised holdings at **www.genealogy.nationalarchives.ie** is a database entitled 'Prerogative and diocesan copies of some wills and indexes to others, 1596–1858'. This includes surviving indexes to wills which did not survive 1922, but also some copies of wills that have survived from the prerogative court (covering 1664–84, 1706–08, 1726–8, 1728–9, 1777, 1813 and 1834) and for the Diocesan Courts of Connor (1818–20, 1853–8) and Down (1850–8).

For the north, many surviving pre-1858 indexes have been integrated into PRONI's free 'Name Search' database (p.66). If a surviving copy of the will exists, and it is held at PRONI, this is stated alongside the index entry.

Various indexes and abridgements have survived which were created for the rest of the records prior to their destruction, many of which are hosted on sites such as Findmypast and Ancestry (p.14). They will in most cases note the names of those who left estate or who were granted administrative bonds. It may not be much, but they can at least help to confirm the period when an ancestor might have passed away.

Many transcripts and abstracts of wills were also compiled by various folk prior to the Four Courts fire, and a useful guide summarising some of these is available on the FamilySearch website at **www.familysearch. org/wiki/en/Ireland_Probate_Records**, noting collections compiled by Sir William Betham, Sir John Bernard Burke, Wallace Clare, Rev. William Carrigan, Philip Crosslé, and others.

The Registry of Deeds, Dublin: Abstracts of Wills (3 vols: 1708–45, 1746–85, 1785–1832), also notes many cases where wills were recorded within the Registry of Deeds (p.125), which can often contain useful information about property. Copies of these can be found in many libraries, but the Irish Manuscripts Commission (p.11) hosts free-to-access digitised editions, whilst Ancestry also offers a searchable database version of the first two volumes.

A typical example of an entry can be seen in the abstract created for a memorial dated 7 September 1809 for a John Cockran, carpenter, who lived at Mallow Lane in the North Liberties of the city of Cork:

> To my wife Mary Cockran, alias Heaphy, my house in Mallow Lane with the concerns thereunto, with the furniture, which I hold from Hariat Exham under a lease for 300 years, as long as she remains unmarried, paying to my eldest son Corns. Cockran £73. 4. 0d. which he had advanced at various times for the support of my family at fifteen pounds per annum. Exors. My son Corns. Cockran, and John McGown, clothier, Blackpool.
> Witnesses: Wm Cochran and David Condon.

Additional details at the end of the entry can allow users to locate the full memorial within the Registry of Deeds.

### Post-1857 probate records

After 1858, the situation improves somewhat. A new civil court-based Principal Registry (now called the Probate Office; **www.courts.ie/probate**) was established in Dublin to oversee a network of District Registries, the number of which has varied across time. Surviving copies of original records from the Principal Registry since 1904, and from most District Registries since 1900, are held at the National Archives in Dublin, as are copy will books with transcripts of most wills from the southern-based District Registries from 1858 onwards.

The NAI's genealogy records website hosts a database entitled 'Will Registers 1858–1900' at **http://census.nationalarchives.ie/search/wr/home.jsp**, which includes 550,000 copies of wills from the District Registries in the south, the largest collection of material to have survived for that period. The records for the Principal Registry in Dublin prior to 1904 have sadly not survived.

However, from 1858 an annual 'Calendar of Grants of Probate of Wills and Letters of Administration made in the Principal Registry and its District Registries' was established, recording short abridgements of each successful court judgement, indexed under the name of the deceased in alphabetical order. From 1858 to 1867 there were two annual volumes produced, one for wills, the other for administrations, but from 1868 onwards both were recorded in a single annual volume. The calendar abridgements note the name of the deceased, the executors (including any relationship between them and the deceased), the date of death, the date for the grant of probate or administration, and the estate's value. A consolidated index also survives, covering 1857–77, which notes the name of the deceased, the District Registry where the cases were held, and whether the record generated concerned the probate of a will or the administration of an intestate person. Following Partition, separate calendar volumes were created for Northern Ireland.

The NAI's set of calendar abridgements for the whole of Ireland go up to 1917, and for the Republic from 1918 to 1982 (with a gap for some holdings from 1920 to 22). These are accessible from 1858 to 1920 at **www.willcalendars.nationalarchives.ie** and via the National Archives catalogue from 1923 to 1982 on its main website.

In the north, prior to Partition in 1921, there were three District Registries, located at Armagh, Londonderry and Belfast. The Armagh Registry was abolished following Partition, but when it existed it administered to testators in counties Armagh, Fermanagh, Louth, Monaghan and Tyrone (excluding those resident within the baronies of Strabane and Omagh in Tyrone).

The surviving records from the three northern District Registries have been placed into a PRONI hosted database covering the period from 1858 to 1965. Over 93,000 surviving transcripts of wills and admon documents made by the District Registries have also been digitised and made free to view, for the following periods:

- Belfast        1858–1909
- Armagh       1858–1918
- Londonderry   1858–1899

There are many instances of people from the Republic of Ireland included in the PRONI database, who were resident within the areas covered by the northern registries. If I search for the town of Drogheda, for example, some 651 entries are flagged up. Most are prior to 1922, such as that for a Peter Bannon of Cooleys Street, Drogheda, who died on 13 March 1878 and whose estate was taken through the Armagh court on 2 April 1878 by a merchant named William Bannon of the town's West Street, with a copy of the will also made available on the site. However, even beyond

Partition, entries can be found; for example, on 29 June 1943, the estate of a Mary Knox of 9 St Peter's Place, Drogheda, and of 30 Ormond Road, Rathmines, Dublin, was taken through the court at Belfast by a Dudley Persse, insurance agent, and a grant of probate issued for her estate, valued at £113 2s.

Conversely, people resident in the north could have their probate cases handled at the Principal Registry in Dublin prior to Partition, and so it is also worth checking the all-Ireland indexes on **www.willcalendars. nationalarchives.ie** as well as the PRONI database. The following example is for my four times great-grandfather John Bill, from Doagh in County Antrim:

> BILL John [524] 4 September Probate of the Wil [*sic*] of John Bill late of Ballyvoy Doagh County Antrim Farmer who died 25 July 1900 granted at Dublin to William Bryson and John Hill Farmers Effects £50

A copy of John's will has not survived, whilst this calendar entry is not located on PRONI's website, making this the only surviving entry for the event.

Copies of most surviving wills in the Republic can be ordered from the NAI via an online application form accessible through its 'Guide to testamentary records' page (see p.121), although those from the most recent twenty years will still be held by the courts.

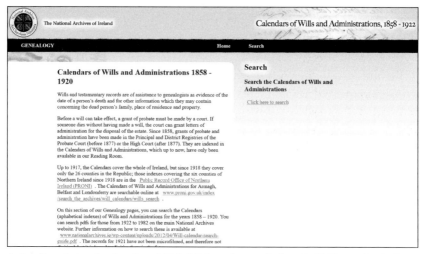

*Ireland's probate calendars from 1858–1920 can be searched on the NAI records platform. Later wills for the Republic can be searched through the NAI catalogue.*

Copies of Northern Irish wills not available online can be consulted at PRONI, with bound calendar volumes available in the Public Search Room. Original wills from the most recent seven years will still be at the courts. An information leaflet for PRONI's enquiry and copy service is available at **www.nidirect.gov.uk/articles/proni-enquiry-service**.

## The Registry of Deeds

Historically there have been two main systems for land registration in Ireland, the Registry of Deeds, established in 1708, and the later Land Registry (p.137), established in 1892. Both remain in use to this day, north and south of the border.

The Registry of Deeds is one of the most important family history resources for pre-civil registration Irish research. Its records concern only a small part of the population, but even where family members are not named, it can still provide fascinating contextual information about an area where they once lived, and the dealings of landowners from whom properties may have been leased.

Following the Cromwellian and Williamite campaigns of the seventeenth century, and the massive seizures of land from Irish Catholics, the Registry was created in 1708 as a means to help Protestant settlers adhering to the Church of Ireland to register title to the lands to which they had come into possession – a process which was entirely voluntary. Prior to this, and indeed even after its establishment, deeds could be recorded through other mechanisms, such as through the manorial courts, where they existed, although very few earlier examples have survived. Land with leases shorter than twenty-two years could not be registered in the Registry until late in the eighteenth century, discriminating against those prevented from holding such agreements by the Penal Laws (p.22)

By the late eighteenth century and the early nineteenth century, Presbyterians and Roman Catholics became better represented within the Registry's pages, following the relaxation of the Penal Laws and the improvements in access to property ownership. Amongst the many transactions that the Registry holds are details of deeds conveying interests in properties from transactions such as sales, mortgages, leases, marriage settlements and wills.

The registration system introduced was fairly straightforward. A deed concerning a property transaction would be signed by both parties to the agreement, and then witnessed. An abridged copy of this was then created, called a 'memorial', with indentured copies provided to both parties. The memorial was verified by a Justice of the Peace, witnessed, and then recorded into the register held in Dublin, and the original memorials filed away for safekeeping. Volumes of memorials transcriptions were kept for easy access, and it is these that we can today access for our research.

An interesting article about the very first memorial to be recorded on 29 March 1708, concerning a lease and release granted by the Earl of Bellomont to Connell Vereker, can be read on the website of the Property Registration Authority (p.10) at **www.prai.ie/blog-no-1-memorial-no-one**, describing the registration process in detail.

The Registry itself is not the easiest to use, with limited indexing, but with perseverance it can yield results. There are two main indexes available to assist. Whichever you choose to use, you need to locate the relevant entry, note down the Transcript Book volume number, the page number and the number of the relevant memorial, before you can consult the original entry for the deed of interest.

The 'Townlands Index' notes deeds under the names of the townlands in which a property is located. From 1708 to 1828 the Townlands Index is arranged by county, with each volume arranging townlands in alphabetical sections. However, the townlands are not arranged alphabetically within the section for that letter, meaning that you may need to look through the entire section to find the area of interest – and it may well be recorded more than once. For example, Buncarrigg may well be listed before Ballymacushan, and then pop up again after.

On another front, you should also be prepared to see the same townland spelt in many different ways, even within the same index volume. Take, for example, the townland of Tybroughney, within the civil parish of the same name in the Barony of Iverk, County Kilkenny. Within the Townlands Index for the county in the volume covering 1895–9 there are nine entries indexed for this barony under the letter T, with six naming variations given for this particular townland:

| Lands | Parish | Grantors | Grantees | Year of Registry | No. of File and Volume of Transcript and Abstract Book | No. of Memorial and Page of Transcript Book | Page of Day Book |
|-------|--------|----------|----------|------------------|--------------------------------------------------------|---------------------------------------------|------------------|
| Tybroughney Tyberaghy Tybraghy | | Power, Nicholas A. & Al. | Baine, John & others | 1889 | 4 | 39 | 107 |
| Tyrbroughney | | Power, Nicholas A. | Power, Alfred R. | 1889 | 27 | 133 | 876 |
| Tyberaghy Tibraghy | | Power, Alfred R. & others | Gyles, Walter & Ann | 1889 | 28 | 118 | 908 |

As can be seen, beside each townland name there will be a short reference, providing the name of the grantor and grantee, the volume number, the relevant memorial number and the page number.

From 1828, the county volumes are further divided by baronies (p.32), and there are separate indexes for cities and counties corporate (p.31), such as Athlone, Carrickfergus, Sligo, Tralee, and Wexford, with entries arranged by street name, rather than townland.

Use of the separate 'Names Index' is handy if you have an ancestor with a rare surname, but it can be quite time consuming for more common names such as Smith. The names indexed are those of the grantor in a transaction, the person conveying a property through a sale or leasehold, as opposed to the grantee in receipt of it. Through this index, entries from 1708 to 1833 are structured in alphabetical order, offering the grantor's name, volume number, page number and memorial reference, but without any description of the property in question; from 1833 onwards the county for the property in question is recorded also.

There is no index to grantees, although this is something that the ongoing volunteer-based Registry of Deeds Index Project Ireland at **https://irishdeedsindex.net** is currently addressing, offering a further way to try to locate entries of interest.

Original copies of the records in the Registry of Deeds can be accessed at the PRA in Dublin (**www.prai.ie**). Its website has a dedicated section at **www.prai.ie/registry-of-deeds-services/#records** describing the records held, and offering the following online indexes:

| | | |
|---|---|---|
| Names Index List | 1708–1969 | Grantors' names |
| Microfilm List | 1930–2018 | A guide to post-1930 memorials |
| Transcript Book List | 1708–1832 | Detailing volume numbers |
| Transcript Book List | 1833–1960 | Detailing volume numbers |
| Abstract Books List | 1833–1969 | Volume numbers for abridgement books |
| Townlands Index List | 1708–1969 | Townlands Index |

All pre-1833 searches must be carried out at the facility, with fees charged for the service, as well as for official searches carried out by staff, as detailed on the website.

However, the majority of the records on microfilm from 1708 to 1929 have been digitised and made available on the FamilySearch website, through its catalogue at **https://familysearch.org/search/catalog/185720**. This hosts all the relevant microfilms, including Grantors Indexes (Names Indexes) arranged in alphabetical order, and within concurrent chronological periods, followed by Land Indexes (Townlands Indexes) arranged in a similar order. The microfilms for the deeds themselves are the final records catalogued on the page, arranged both chronologically and by volume number.

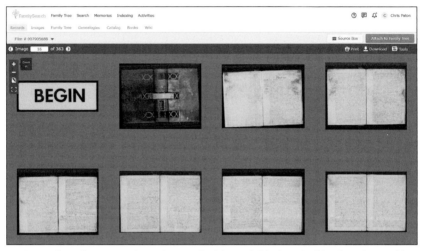

*Registry of Deeds memorials can be searched through black and white digital microfilms hosted on FamilySearch, although the earlier records may be difficult to read online.*

To access the records you must register with the site first and then log in. Most of the records can be viewed on your computer, by clicking on the camera icon at the end of the relevant listing; if you are not signed in to your account, the camera symbol may be replaced with one showing it to be 'locked'. Once viewed, relevant entries can be downloaded and saved to your computer, or printed off.

Let us take for example the Breen family of the townland of Rathduff in the civil parish of Killann, County Wexford, for which I wish to locate any entries in the early 1880s. The first I need to know is in which barony the parish of Killann is based. Using the various tools discussed on p.38, I quickly discover that the relevant barony involved is Bantry. On FamilySearch, I now need to search for the Land Indexes, and soon find the link to the correct microfilm:

| Note | Location | Collection/Shelf | Film | DGS | Format |
|---|---|---|---|---|---|
| Place name index by county, Wexford and Wicklow 1880–1884 | Granite Mountain Record Vault | British | 100707 | 8078600 | Camera icon |

This is now the fiddly bit. Clicking on the camera icon takes me to the digital microfilm, which starts with indexes for Volume 1, County Wexford. The contents list on page 8 shows that the records are arranged by barony in the following order:

| | |
|---|---|
| Barony of Ballaghkeene, North and South | p.1 |
| Barony of Bantry | p.59 |
| Barony of Bargy | p.114 |
| Barony of Forth | p.188 |

I therefore need to skip forward a few pages to page 59 in the printed volume, which is actually at page 36 on the microfilm, as the volume was photographed with two facing pages at a time. The Land Index for this barony is arranged alphabetically, so I need to skip forward to the index page for place names beginning with R, which I can finally find at page 94 in the volume (page 54 of the microfilm).

I can now see a long list of place names beginning with R. They are not arranged in any particular order, and several townland names are repeatedly noted, for different transactions. There are in fact fourteen mentions of Rathduff (noted as Rathduff and Rathduffe) across two pages, but only one mentions the surname Breen as either a Grantor or Grantee – in this case, for both:

| Lands | Parish | Grantor | Grantee | Year of Registry | No. of File and Volume of Transcript and Abstract Book | No. of Memorial and Page of Transcript Book | Page of Day Book |
|---|---|---|---|---|---|---|---|
| Rathduff | | Charles Breen | Patrick Breen | 1880 | 26 | 30 | 672 |

(Source: Place name index by county, Wexford and Wicklow 1880–1884 **www.familysearch. org/ark:/61903/3:1:3Q9M-CSNX-XSQV-6?i=53&cat=185720**)

The next stage is to look up the original record. I know that the year in question is 1880, and the volume involved is 26. The relevant microfilm for this is soon identified on Family Search

| Note | Location | Collection/Shelf | Film | DGS | Format |
|------|----------|------------------|------|-----|--------|
| Deeds, etc., v. 26–29 1880 | Granite Mountain Record Vault | British | 534514 | 8093735 | Camera icon |

Clicking on the camera icon for this microfilm takes me to the original book. The digital microfilm has four volumes (26–29), but I need the first. From the Land Index, I know that the memorial number I need is 30, and that it is on page 672 of the volume. Frustratingly I cannot see the page numbers on this volume, but the memorials are in numerical order, so starting from the beginning, I soon find the entry numbered 30, and it is indeed a transaction from a 'Breen' to a 'Breen'. I can now read the record, and soon discover that it is a memorial of an indenture from a Charles Breen of Curragraigue to his son, Patrick Breen of Milltown, concerning the lands of Milltown, otherwise known as Rathduff or Raheenfinch. This particular memorial can be viewed at **www.familysearch.org/ark:/61903/3:1:3Q9M-CSJ4-W9NH-G?i=17&cat=185720**. Of course, now that I know of two possible name variants for the townland, it is probably worth going back to the Land Index again to see if there are any other references to the family using Milltown or Raheenfinch as the townland name.

It should be noted that the black and white microfilming by FamilySearch that took place was not perfect, with parts of some volumes difficult to read, with poor cropping, and in some instances, illegibility, due to the poor quality of the original source material, particularly with the earlier volumes. You may still need, or wish, to see the originals in Dublin.

Not everyone will be mentioned in the Registry of Deeds, but it is certainly always worth searching for members of your family and for the townlands of interest within it.

The all-Ireland Registry of Deeds memorials from 1708 to 1922 are also freely available to consult on microfilm at PRONI, as are paper indexes from 1923 to 1989 for Northern Irish registered entries post-Partition.

## Landowners in Ireland 1876

One further nineteenth-century exercise worth mentioning was the survey entitled 'A Return of Owners of Land of One Acre and Upwards in the Several Counties, Counties of Cities, and Counties of Towns of Ireland', published in 1876 as part of a wider United Kingdom-based survey. This noted the number and names of 32,614 people who held land of one statute acre or more, whether it was built upon or not. This included lessees for terms exceeding ninety-nine years or with a right of perpetual renewal, as well as the numbers of land owners with lands of less than an acre, but without noting their names. Those recorded are listed alphabetically by county, with the entries noting the size of their holdings and its rateable value.

The records were published and can be consulted in many libraries. The *Fáilte Romhat* platform also hosts a free-to-access version online at **www.failteromhat.com/lo1876.htm**, whilst *The Great Landowners of Great Britain and Ireland*, published in 1883, is also freely available on Google Books at **www.google.co.uk/books/edition/The_Great_Landowners_of_Great_Britain_an/99hGAAAAIAAJ**, detailing holders of the larger estates.

## Irish Land Commission

In the aftermath of the Famine, many landed estate landowners were forced to sell off their estates; they were no longer a cash cow but a major drain on their remaining depleted resources. To assist them in doing so, the Encumbered Estates Acts of 1848 and 1849 were passed by the British government to permit the state to buy up such lands and to then redistribute them with a new title. This was done first through the Encumbered Estate Court from 1849, the Landed Estates Court from 1852, and then the Land Judges Court from 1877. From 1870, the Landlord and Tenant (Ireland) Act had also made it theoretically possible for tenants to purchase property from their landlords, but there was little take up. The rental records generated as part of the sales processes have previously been discussed on p.113, whilst the sales themselves may be noted in the Registry of Deeds.

In 1879, the Land War then exploded in Ireland, with the main issues being how to address the parasitical nature of landlordism, with demands for fair rent, better security of tenure, and an improved right to buy. In response, the Land Law (Ireland) Act 1881 was passed by the British government, establishing a new Irish Land Commission, which initially sought to intervene in the rents issue, but which also assumed the work of the Landed Estates Courts. The Commission soon also took on the role of a tenancy purchasing commission, assisting those wishing to buy their holdings outright with loans to be repaid over thirty-five years at 5 per cent interest, and granting tenants 'vesting orders' for their new holdings, essentially title deeds in their name, clear of any previous burdens or encumbrances. The scheme was further extended with the Purchase of Land (Ireland) Act in 1885, which extended loans repayments to over forty-nine years, and again in 1889.

To give an example of how useful this scheme was for the family historian, I was able to locate a memorial from 1892 within the Registry of Deeds concerning the purchase of the farm in County Kilkenny, on the border with Tipperary, belonging to my wife's great-grandmother Bridget Prendergast, at Killonerry townland (p.96). This showed that in August 1892, Bridget, noted as the widow of Thomas Prendergast, purchased the farm through the Court of the Irish Land Commission from the estate of the Earl of Bessborough:

COURT OF THE IRISH LAND COMMISSION
LAND PURCHASE (IRELAND) ACTS, 1870 TO 1891.
Record Number 522.
Before MR. COMMISSIONER MACCARTHY.

Tuesday the Second day of August, One Thousand Eight Hundred and Ninety-two.

In the Matter of the Estate of THE RIGHT HONOURABLE GEORGE BRABAZON, EARL OF BESSBOROUGH, a Vendor of Land.

IT IS ORDERED by the Irish Land Commission pursuant to the powers vested in them by the Land Purchase (Ireland) Acts, 1870 to 1891, that the Lands and Hereditaments comprised in the Holding described in the Schedule hereto, in the occupation of the Purchasing Tenant therein named (and which have been purchased for the sum therein stated), with the appurtenances, DO VEST, and the same are hereby VESTED in the said Tenant in fee-simple, Subject to and Charged with the repayment to the said Commission of the sum specified in the said Schedule, as having been advanced to them to the said Tenant for the purchase of the said Lands, with interest thereon, by the Annuity in the said Schedule stated, for the Term of Forty-nine years, from the First day of May, One Thousand Eight Hundred and Ninety-two, payable by equal half-yearly payments on each First day of May and First day of November, the first payment thereof to be made on the First day of November next, and Also Charged with interest on the said advance at the rate of three and one eighth per cent per annum, from the Second day of December, One Thousand Eight Hundred and Ninety-one, to the First day of May, One Thousand Eight Hundred and Ninety-two, and payable with the first instalment of the said Annuity, but freed from all other charges.

SCHEDULE ABOVE REFERRED TO.

Name of Purchasing Tenant – BRIDGET PRENDERGAST.
Postal Address – Killonerry, Carrick-on-Suir, County Tipperary.
Description – Widow.
Amount of Purchase Money – Two Thousand Six Hundred and Fifty Pounds.
Sum advanced to the said Tenant for the purchase of her Holding – Two Thousand Six Hundred and Fifty Pounds.
Annuity payable for Forty-nine years – One Hundred and Six Pounds.

Description of Holding – That part of the Lands of Killonerry, containing One Hundred and Twenty-eight Acres Two Roods and Twenty-eight Perches, statute measure or thereabouts, situate in the Barony of Iverk, and County of Kilkenny, as held by the said Tenant at the date of the making of the advance, as Tenant to the said Vendor, under Lease dated Fourth May, One Thousand Eight Hundred and Sixty-eight, and made between the Right Honourable John George Brabazon, late Earl of Bessborough, of the one Part, and Thomas Prendergast, of the other Part, for Thirty-one years from the First November, One Thousand Eight Hundred and Sixty-seven.

The record not only noted Bridget's purchase of the farm, it also confirms a previous thirty-one-year lease held by her husband from the Earl of Bessborough, dating from 1867, and the extent of the farm holding, which matches that as described earlier in Griffith's Valuation (p.91).

Further measures to extend the right to buy for tenants were implemented by the Commission through the Land Purchase (Ireland) Act 1903, also known as Wyndham's Act, which led to loan repayments to be repaid over sixty-eight and a half years at 3.25 per cent and the Land Purchase (Ireland) Act 1909, better known as Birrel's Act.

The files of the Irish Land Commission have a massive potential for genealogists, and house and land historians; they contain a great deal of supporting material for the sales that were facilitated, including title deeds, copies of wills, estate plans and considerably more, which landowners were required to submit to establish initial proof of ownership prior to a sale. At the time of writing, however, a great problem is that the records for the Republic of Ireland are largely not open to public access.

Although not fully catalogued, the material within the Commission's Records Branch have been at least surveyed to an extent by Edward Keane from the National Library of Ireland for properties between 1881 and 1909, with the indexes accessible at the facility for consultation. A card index exists for 9,343 estates in Ireland, available in two parts – a 'Topographical Index', listing the barony, county and vendors' names, and a 'Name Index', detailing the vendor's name, the location of the estate, and the estate's number. Using these, some further details can be found in bound volumes providing information about the existence of documents, if not the documents themselves. Separate materials concerning the Commission's Administration Branch are documented on a catalogue held on site at the National Archives of Ireland. The original material, however, for both the Records Branch and the Administrative Branch, cannot be consulted at present for the apparent reason that they contain private and sensitive information.

Following Partition, the Land Commission's historic files were divided into those for Northern Ireland and those for the new Free State. The Commission in the south was reconstituted from 1923, and continued with its work through several further reforms until 31 March 1999, at which point the Commission was finally dissolved and its records transferred to the Department of Agriculture. Since then, nothing has happened to them, with no cataloguing or any conservation work carried out, with the records essentially locked away in a warehouse in Portlaoise. If there are further records concerning Bridget's purchase of Killonerry Farm in 1892, for now, they are gathering dust on a shelf, hiding within one of 50,000 boxes of material from the Commission's Records Branch collection. A useful article from Fiona Fitzsimons about the zombie like status of these records was published in *History Ireland*, Jan/Feb 2014, Volume 22, available online at **www.historyireland.com/ volume-22/records-irish-land-commission**.

In this regard, from a northern perspective, Partition has actually come to the rescue for those seeking access to the equivalent records for Northern Ireland. Following the creation of Northern Ireland in 1921, the Land Commission in the north was reconstituted as the Land Purchase Commission (NI). There were two further land acts passed, the Northern Ireland Land Acts of 1925 and 1929, before the Commission was finally disbanded on 1 April 1937, following the passage of the Northern Ireland Land Purchase (Winding Up) Act 1935. At this point, the jurisdiction of the Commission was passed to the Chancery Judge of the High Court of Justice, and the historic records were transferred to the Public Record

Office of Northern Ireland. These can now be accessed at PRONI under catalogue holdings LR1 and LR2.

To locate records of interest, you will need to perform the following search procedure:

- Track the pattern of ownership through the Valuation Revision Books on the PRONI website (p.97), until the point when the holding of interest is noted as being held 'in fee' (outright ownership), and with a stamp denoting 'L.A.P.' ('Land Act Purchase'). The name of the prior owner will be scored out, and a date given in the right-hand margin stating when the purchase occurred. In some cases, you may have to consult the book prior to that showing the land held 'in fee' for the name of the former owner.
- Once you have the previous owner's name, consult PRONI's online 'Guide to Land Registry index' at **www.nidirect.gov.uk/publications/ guide-land-registry-index**. This index lists all estate and property owners in alphabetical order who sold their land through the Commission, providing their Surname, First Name, County, Box number, Code (NI, LJ or EC), and Record Number. The key detail needed from this is the box number, which when identified can allow you to find the relevant record from the catalogue.
- On the PRONI catalogue, access the 'Browse' function from the top right corner of the page. In the search box presented, now type in LR1/ followed by the box number to form a single reference (e.g. LR1/458) and click 'Search'.
- On the list of results returned, click on the reference again under the PRONI Reference column on the left. A list of potential papers from that box should be returned now, possibly subdivided further into different transactions (e.g. LR1/458/1, LR1/458/2, etc.). Clicking on this should reveal information of records that can be called up.

Take, for example, a search for the purchase of a property by John McManus from the townland of Drumhariff within the County Fermanagh parish of Aghalurcher, and poor law union of Lisnaskea. The Valuation Revision Books for the townland for the period from 1899 to 1914 (VAL/12/B/28/5D) note John McManus as the tenant to 'Wm. Brady', whose name is scored out in blue, with the words 'in fee' handwritten beside it, and 'L.A.P.' stamped beside it. The column to the right side of the page notes this transaction to have happened in 1909, with the year handwritten in the same colour as the words 'in fee'.

Now that we know William Brady was the last owner before John McManus used the Land Commission to buy the property for himself, we can consult the Guide to Land Registry index, which brings up only one entry for someone of that name:

| Surname | Forename | County | Box | Code | Record No. |
|---------|----------|--------|-----|------|-----------|
| Brady | Wm | Fermanagh | 619 | EC | 173 |

On the PRONI catalogue, if I select Browse and now carry out a search for the reference LR1/619, I can find the following collection description:

| PRONI Reference | Title/Description | Date | Digital Record |
|-----------------|------------------|------|----------------|
| LR1/619/1 | Name: W. M. Brady, County Fermanagh, Record Number EC173, Box 619 More | 1899–1925 | |

Clicking on the reference in the first column returns the following additional details:

| PRONI Reference | Title/Description | Date | Digital Record |
|-----------------|------------------|------|----------------|
| LR1/619/1/A | Administrative Documents More | 1899–1905 | |
| LR1/619/1/B | Title Deeds [Not received] More | No Date | |
| LR1/619/1/C | Testamentary Papers [Not received] More | No Date | |

If planning a visit to PRONI, I will now have an idea of what I will be able to consult on my trip from this search, and just as importantly, note what is not included.

Further guidance on the background to the records, and their use, is available from PRONI in its information leaflet, 'Family Tree – Land Registry records', accessible at **www.nidirect.gov.uk/publications/family-tree-land-registry-records**.

Another useful resource to help with Land Purchase Commission research in Northern Ireland is the *Belfast Gazette* newspaper, which commenced publication in the north as a successor to the *Dublin Gazette* following Partition, and which is freely available online at **www.thegazettes.co.uk**. The title regularly advertised land and estates to be acquired by the Commission, and included details on tenants and holdings within them for public comment.

For example, in an edition dated 8 February 1929, there is a notice from the Land Purchase Commission advertising a provisional list of tenants and twenty-nine holdings on the estate of a widow named Elizabeth Dorothea Shaw Tener, in the townlands of Knockavaddy and

Moneygaragh, in the barony of Upper Dungannon, County Tyrone. The land was soon to be vested in the Commission, which was providing an opportunity for any member of the public to object to the description of the holdings, or to advise of any omissions from, or objections to, the list, within a month of the publication date.

The following details for the first tenant's holding provides an example of the information returned:

| Name of Tenant | Postal Address | Barony | Townland | Reference No. on Map Filed in Land Purchase Commission | Area A. R. P. | Rent £. s. d. | Standard Purchase Annuity if Land Becomes Vested | Standard Price if Land Becomes Vested |
|---|---|---|---|---|---|---|---|---|
| ing subject to a Judicial Rent fixed before the 16th August, 1896. | | | | | | | | |
| Bernard McCormick | Knockavaddy, Rock, Dungannon, Co. Tyrone | Upper Dungannon | Knockavaddy | 7 | 8 0 25 | 4 0 0 | 2 8 2 | 61 4 7 |

The subsequent holdings are grouped together according to holdings subject to a judicial rent fixed between 15 August 1896 and 16 August 1911, those with rents fixed after 15 August 1911, and additional holdings subject to 'Rents other than Judicial Rents'. From a genealogical point of view there are some useful biographical details for some of the female tenants holding lots, with two described as widows, one as a spinster, and a further woman, Bridget Hayden, listed as the 'wife of Dominic Hayden'.

In this example, the information offered is dated later than that from the final available Valuation Revision Book online from PRONI, which covers the period from 1914 to 1923 (VAL/12/B/37/17F). In the *Gazette* advertisement, the estate is noted as held by a widow named Elizabeth Dorothea Shaw Tener, but in the preceding Valuation Revision Book the immediate lessor for the lands is instead shown as Edward S. Tener, her husband, who had died in November 1915.

### The Land Registry

The Land Registry was introduced in 1892 as a means to provide a more flexible title registration system than the more limited voluntary-based Registry of Deeds system could offer. This was implemented following the passing of the Registration of Title Act 1891. As with everything else on the island, the advent of Partition led to the work of the Land Registry being split, with both agencies north and south evolving along separate lines since then.

The Land Registry for the Republic of Ireland can be accessed at the PRA offices in Dublin, Roscommon and Waterford (p.10). The authority's website at **www.prai.ie/land-registry-services** provides a handy overview of the registration process, a glossary of terms commonly found in the documents, and details on how to access the public register for a fee at its offices.

In addition, a useful interactive map at **www.landdirect.ie** allows you to search for properties that have been included in the Land Registry. Based on the modern Ordnance Survey Ireland map (p.142) this allows you to zoom in and see an overlay of property boundaries for all those registered with titles. Searches will reveal whether information is held about the property on the Land Registry (if not you will need to consult the Registry of Deeds), and if so, whether it is held by leasehold or as a freehold. The size of the holding will also be noted, and the relevant Folio number. A copy of the full Folio, if ordered from the service, will include three parts: a description of the property, details on ownership, and any known burdens or liabilities affecting the holding (such as a right of way across the land).

Following Partition, a separate Land Registry has been in operation in Northern Ireland, as with the separate series of Registry of Deeds memorials, both of which are managed by Land and Property Services (p.10), which operates five customer services facilities to provide access at Ballymena, Belfast, Craigavon, Omagh and Londonderry. In 1951, a Statutory Charge Register was also established, for purchasers to be able to check in advance if any restrictions exist concerning a property prior to purchase. Further information on access to the Registry of Deeds and Land Registry services are available on the LPS site at **www.nidirect.gov. uk/information-and-services/buying-your-home/land-and-property-registers**.

In both the Republic of Ireland and Northern Ireland it is the intention that in the future the Registry of Deeds will be phased out, with all property transactions recorded on their respective Land Registries.

### Church land commissions

In 1711, the Church of Ireland was permitted a new funding arrangement by the Crown to build churches and accommodation for ministers on lands acquired for its use, through a newly established body called the Board of First Fruits (so called from the pre-Reformation tax of 'first fruits' and 'twentieth parts' initially paid to the Papacy, and then to the Crown). In addition to new funding granted by the Crown, the Church had the right to levy a parish cess, or tax, for the upkeep of its ecclesiastical buildings, and also earned a regular income from the tithes due to it (p.86).

The Church Temporalities (Ireland) Act 1833 introduced many reforms to the structure and financing of the Anglican Church, which included the right for its tenants to acquire their holdings for a fixed rent, and the abolition of the parish cess in favour of a new tax on clerical income. The funds obtained from this and other sources was to now be administered by a new body, the Board of Ecclesiastical Commissioners, which replaced the Board of First Fruits. Annual reports from the Board from 1835 to 1869 can be consulted on the DIPPAM website at **www. dippam.ac.uk**.

Following the Act to disestablish the Church of Ireland as the state church in 1869, a new body was set up, the Commission of Church Temporalities, which oversaw the sale of lands and property owned by the church. One of the many functions of this Commission was to offer some 11,000 tenants the right to purchase their holdings. The functions of the Commission were eventually transferred in 1881 to the Irish Land Commission (p.131).

'The Report of the Commissioners of Church Temporalities in for the Period 1869-80' is available on the Internet Archive at **https://archive. org/details/op1251039-1001**. Appendix 12 of this publication includes a fairly extensive 'Schedules of Sales and Yearly Tenures, arranged by diocese', which lists the following details for each plot of land sold in this period:

- Name of purchasers
- The Benefice and Denomination of Land Sold
- County and Barony
- Date of Sale
- Area of Holding
- Tenement Valuation
- Annual Rent
- Purchase Money: Gross Amount, Paid in Cash, Secured by Mortgage

PRONI holds many records from the Commission, which it has catalogued under FIN/10/10, with the majority of documents concerning mortgages. The archive's leaflet, 'Local History 9: The Commissioners of Church Temporalities in Ireland' (FIN/10/10), outlines further details at **www.nidirect.gov.uk/articles/local-history-series**.

Some solicitors' department records from 1834 to 1879 are also held by the Representative Church Body Library in Dublin (**www.ireland. anglican.org/about/rcb-library**), catalogued under MS585.

## Chapter 7

# A SENSE OF PLACE

Understanding who lived in a place at any one time, and who actually owned their properties or rented them, are some of the biggest challenges that we will come across in our ancestral research. There is one further important factor to try to take into account, however, and that is to gain an understanding of the wider contemporary environments within which they once lived.

Although I was born in Northern Ireland in 1970, I was almost immediately whisked across to Scotland for four years, and then down to England for another four, before returning to live again in the County Antrim town of Carrickfergus. From 1979 to 1991 I spent the next twelve years of my childhood and early adult life in 'Carrick' as it was called, attending primary school, grammar school and then commuting for two years to the University of Ulster in Belfast to study an HND course in design and communication. It was a great place to grow up, but the Carrickfergus in which I was raised no longer exists. The town of Carrickfergus itself still exists, of course – but not *my* Carrick.

Every community in the country is under constant change – new industries come and go, new communications are opened and closed, and different families and communities within the fabric of the town move in or move away. The town's West Street, once packed with shoppers fetching their daily 'messages' is now a virtual ghost town, as out-of-town supermarkets have sucked the life from the once vibrant urban centre. The old mills and factories have all closed, or have been converted into accommodation blocks, and many of the residents in Carrick now live there as a convenient place for the daily commute to and from Belfast, which lies just 9 miles further along the shore of Belfast Lough. Indeed, so aware have I been of the dramatic nature of the changes in the town that I have actually written up an extensive account

*Carrickfergus Castle in County Antrim.*

of my childhood there for my children, detailing the story of the town that I lived in, from an era now long gone.

The Carrickfergus I grew up in was, in turn, also quite different to the place where my father grew up. As previously noted in the introduction to this book, when he was a small child, he lived in the second house along a small road called Robinson's Row (p.8) in the town's Joymount district, with my Scottish grandmother and his siblings. At that time, in the 1950s, the main coast road was located just a few feet down from the house, bounded on its far side by the town's old sea wall, and on stormy nights the spray from the waves would reach the windows of their house. In 1979, however, when we returned from England to live in my grandmother's house (she having passed away the previous year and left the house to my father), there was no longer a coast road at the bottom of Robinson's Row. In the 1960s, a massive project to reclaim land alongside the shore led to the creation of a new coast road called the Marine Highway, and a huge garden complex called the Marine Gardens, both of which now stand between the old row of houses and Belfast Lough.

Places change, communities change, and indeed, the very 'vibe' of a place changes. Whilst we can put names to people and identify where they stayed, and perhaps even touch the fabric of buildings once inhabited, it is difficult to actually gain a sense of the place from times past.

Nevertheless, there are certainly a variety of resources which exist that can help us to determine the make-up of communities past, including maps, parish records, gazetteers and more. In this chapter I will look at some of the most useful.

### Irish Historic Towns Atlas

There are various mapping resources which can help us to determine how an area once looked, and which, when compared with others in a chronological order, can help to build up a useful visual time line.

If your ancestors lived in an urban setting, some of the best resources for exploring the development of the town or city are the publications of the 'Irish Historic Towns Atlas' project. This was first established by the Royal Irish Academy (**www.ria.ie**) in 1981 to record the developments of Irish towns across the island, and at the time of writing has published some twenty-seven volumes, with plenty more under preparation. The towns and cities already covered include Kildare, Carrickfergus, Bandon, Kells, Mullingar, Athlone, Maynooth, Downpatrick, Bray, Kilkenny, Dublin, Belfast, Fethard, Trim, Derry, Dundalk, Armagh, Tuam, Limerick, Longford, Carlingford, Sligo, Ennis and Youghal.

With a strong family connection to Belfast, I purchased the relevant pack for the development of the city from the years 1840–1900. This was in fact Volume 17 of the run, and the second covering Belfast, an earlier pack having previously focused on the pre-1840 period. In the later volume there is a detailed list of all the streets to have come and gone in the city, as well as lists of institutions such as schools, churches and industries and more. Most importantly, there is a series of reproductions of large scale maps and plates detailing the city within the period, a resource which I use on many occasions for my research.

For further information on the series, and on how to purchase copies, consult the Research Projects section of the Royal Irish Academy website, and its online bookshop.

### Ordnance Survey maps

Although maps of Ireland have been drawn up for centuries, the most comprehensive exercise by far has been the work of the Ordnance Survey, first established in Ireland in 1824, by surveyors from the Royal Engineers under the direction of Colonel Thomas Corby.

Prior to Partition, the work continued to be carried out by the British Ordnance Survey. From 1922, the Ordnance Survey of Northern Ireland (**www.finance-ni.gov.uk/topics/mapping-and-geographic-information**) and the Ordnance Survey of Ireland (**www.osi.ie**) were both established to continue the job of mapping the terrain of the separate jurisdictions.

Most of the maps produced are of the scale of 6 inches to the mile, although in more densely populated areas maps have been produced at 25 inches to the mile. For the Republic of Ireland, the Ordnance Survey website also allows you to view historic nineteenth-century OS maps online. The included maps are presented as follows:

- OSi Cassini 6-inch series (1830s–1930s)
- Historic map 6-inch colour (1837–1842)
- Historic Map 6-inch Black & White (1837–1842)
- Historic Map 25-inch (1888–1913)

In addition to the current maps, the site also provides aerial photographic surveys for the whole of the Republic from 1995 (black and white), 2000, 2005, and 2005–12.

For Northern Ireland you can access the modern OSNI map via the Spatial NI platform at **https://maps.spatialni.gov.uk**. This provides many possible overlays of mapping and photographic data, including Historic Industrial Land Use, townland boundaries, wards (1993), local government districts (2012), Historic Environment sites and monuments, listed buildings, areas of significance and historic parks, an OSNI gazetteer, orthophotography (aerial photography) and more.

Historic OS maps online are found through the PRONI Historical Maps Viewer at **www.nidirect.gov.uk/information-and-services/search-archives-online/proni-historical-maps-viewer**. This provides free access to the following historic maps:

- Edition 1 (1832 to 1846)
- Edition 2 (1846 to 1862)
- Edition 3 (1900 to 1907)
- Edition 4 (1905 to 1957)
- Edition 5 (1919 to 1963)
- 6″ Irish Grid (1952 to 1969)
- 1:10,000 metric Irish Grid (1957 to 1986)

Using the search box on this site you can search for an area by townland, parish or town/city name, or with a modern Northern Irish postal address. The widget tools at the top right of the search screen also permits the overlay of a series of 'layers' on to a map, including points of interest (such as courts, churches and schools) and boundary information for counties, parishes and townlands.

Print copies of many OS maps can be purchased via the OS websites themselves, or via Cassini Maps at **www.cassinimaps.co.uk** and Alan Godfrey Maps at **www.alangodfreymaps.co.uk**.

The Ask About Ireland site (p.92) offers many, though not all, of the Ordnance Survey Name Books and Letter Books from the original survey exercise, which were published between 1824 and 1842. Predominantly available for counties in the south, these can be searched by parish at **www. askaboutireland.ie/griffith-valuation/index.xml?action=nblSearch**. The surveyors' books were used to provide standardised spellings for all the areas surveyed, but include some interesting anecdotes and details along the way.

## Ordnance Survey Memoirs

As part of the first Ordnance Survey of Ireland, a series of 'memoirs' or reports were also commissioned to accompany the maps produced. The task of designing the questions to determine the environmental, economic and social information to be presented in these reports fell to Lieutenant Thomas Larcom, assistant to the survey director Colonel Thomas Colby. The effort commenced in the northern part of the country in 1833.

Unfortunately, due to the scheme's vast expense, only one volume was published in the 1830s, that for Templemore parish in County Londonderry (including the city of Londonderry), before the project collapsed a couple of years later. Despite this, a great deal of information had been gathered for many areas of the north, most of which was subsequently deposited with the Royal Irish Academy. The institution holds has a vast collection of drawings, sketches, letters and more generated by the OS team within its special collections. Information on these, and examples, can be viewed at **www.ria.ie/library/catalogues/ special-collections/modern-manuscripts/ordnance-survey-ireland-archive**.

In the 1990s, a programme to publish the surviving material was commenced by the Institute of Irish Studies and Queen's University, Belfast, working in partnership with the Royal Irish Academy. Some forty volumes were produced for the following counties: Antrim (14 volumes), Armagh (a single volume), Donegal (2 volumes), Down (4 volumes), Fermanagh (2 volumes), Londonderry (14 volumes), Tyrone (2 volumes), and Cavan, Leitrim, Louth, Monaghan and Sligo (a single volume for all five counties). The weight of the content available is for counties Antrim and Londonderry, and there are some notable omissions to the parishes available in the volumes for the other counties that were produced – for example, although all of the parishes in Armagh were covered in a single volume, the city of Armagh is not included, as it was never written up by Larcom's original team.

All of these volumes, as well as a comprehensive index to the series created in 2002 by Dr Patrick McWilliams, can be purchased from the Ulster Historical Foundation's bookshop at **www.booksireland.org.uk**. A summary of OS Memoir publications by county, previously published by Queen's University Belfast, is cached on the Internet Archive at **http://bit.ly/OSMcountieslist**, with a further list collated by parish in alphabetical order at **http://bit.ly/OSMparishlist**, listing the volume numbers in which they appear.

The material found within the volumes provides a rich tapestry to set your ancestors lives against, and in some cases, may even name them. In the memoir for Larne and Islandmagee (volume 10), a list of annual migrants to Scotland from 1838 notes a 25-year-old David Gordon, an adherent of the Established Church (Anglican), from the townland of Ballylumford in Islandmagee, who had 'no capital'. This is a strong contender for my own four times great-grandfather of the same name, who later died in Belfast at the stated age of 56 in 1876. Elsewhere in the volume there are other mentions of the Gordon family, including a wonderful description of one of the industries they were employed within:

The sea wrack is used as manure. Some of it is placed behind the fire in the kitchens of the houses at large through the parish. It is produced along the shore of both the sea and the lough. The seaweed called tankle or stem is the best for manure, and the wrack is best for fire. The wrack and seaweed is free to all the inhabitants, except the wrack which sticks on the stones, and this the proprietors of the land adjoining the shore claim, and many of them manufacturing it into kelp, by which some have realised a considerable sum of money. The Laffertys and Gordons with many others have manufactured it extensively every year until 1838, foreign ashes being so cheap. (Islandmagee p.85)

There is also a mention of the townland on Kilcoan, where the only farm held by the Gordons on Islandmagee was located, which notes two members of the family:

In the same townland, at the White House on the lough shore, a vast quantity of human bones and old silver coins of various kinds have been dug up at various times, with horses' bones. Also a battle is supposed to have been fought here on John Gordon's farm. Information obtained from Hugh Laverty and Alexander Gordon. (Islandmagee p.102)

The memoirs provide descriptions of geographical features, such as hills, loughs, bogs and rivers, information on religious worship houses and schools, communications, the use of machinery in the parishes, local history and the social economy, the structures of local government, notes on the great and the good in the parishes, as well as the most notable names. There is also a statistical description of the number of folk residing in each parish, their character and superstitions, as well as lists of those who drowned at sea, emigrated, taught at schools and more. They offer a veritable treasure chest of information for the parish on both the inhabitants and the environment itself.

## Gazetteers, journals and parish histories

There are many contemporary gazetteers and travel journals that have been compiled over the last three centuries which can also help to flesh out the topography of an area across time. There are of course far too many to note here, with many holdings available at the NLI, the Linen Hall Library in Belfast, and in other repositories across the country. Again, John Grenham's *Tracing Your Irish Ancestors* provides an excellent bibliography of titles to be consulted on a county by county basis, and increasingly there are some useful collections appearing online that can be consulted also.

As an instant ready reckoner, a useful resource to consult for place names across Ireland is Samuel Lewis' *The Parliamentary Gazetteer of Ireland: Adapted to the New Poor-law, Franchise, Municipal and Ecclesiastical Arrangements, and Compiled with a Special Reference to the Lines of Railroad and Canal Communication as Existing in 1843–44*. This usefully notes in which parish, barony and county a place will be located, and also provides a brief history and some contemporary information for the larger areas at the time of publication, such as its size in acres, the number of houses and the size of its population. The work can be found online at Google Books (**https://books.google.co.uk**) and via the Internet Archive (**https://archive.org**).

Both of these online library resources are well worth plundering for out of copyright works. Whilst searching for County Antrim resources, for example, I came across a copy of a book from 1873 called *An Historical Account of the MacDonnells of Antrim* by George Hill, which amongst its appendices included a transcript of a late seventeenth-century report by Richard Dobbs, entitled 'A Briefe Description of the County of Antrim, begun the 3rd of May, 1683'. In his coverage of the parish of Islandmagee, Dobbs in fact gave a description of the farm held by my Brown family, for whom Brown's Bay was named at the far north of the parish:

> Now return we again to Portmuck, from whence to the Corran, which is the entrance into Loughlarn, is a very hard shore, except a little Bay called Brown's Bay, clear and sandy, open to the north-west winds, and has in it a little shelter for small boats; we are yet in Island Magee, which affords little or no spring; the poorer people burning (instead of turf and coal) much of their straw in winter time, yet one James Brown who lives at the Bay last mentioned, having a good farm here, has near his house excellent meadow, wherein of late years he has found very good turf, and under that moss clay appears again, which being removed he finds good turf again, and so as he tells me it may be further down.

Dobbs also noted that:

> The northend of this island is sandy, dry, and fit for rabbits; but the people here think that no profit can be made but by ploughing, in which the men spend their whole time, except the summer quarter in providing and bringing home fireing [sic]; and the women theirs, in spinning and making linen cloth, and some ordinary woollen for their family's use. There is a handsome church much out of repair, but no churchmen. A meeting house, all presbiters, all Scotch, not one Irish or English, except a custom house waiter. The Dean of Connor, is vicar.

The Ask About Ireland Reading Room at **www.askaboutireland.ie/ reading-room** contains various digitised eBooks for each county in the Republic of Ireland, including a range of useful contemporary guides. If we look at Donegal, for instance, there is a copy of the 1802 Statistical Survey for the county, Maguire's *History of the Diocese of Raphoe*, a Registry of Deeds (p.125) index for deeds registered in the 1760s and 1770s in the county, and several parish histories. Similarly, if we examine Tipperary we find two volumes of *The Civil Survey A.D. 1654–1656: County of Tipperary*, detailing the land owners in parishes and baronies across the county, noting the size of their holdings and rateable value at that time.

Parish histories are also well worth consulting, not just for a concise summary of an area's history but also for the bibliography of sources from which the account was drawn. Again, if we stick with Islandmagee as a useful example, some time ago I purchased a copy of a book printed in 1979 called *Between Two Revolutions: Islandmagee, County Antrim 1798–1920*, written by Donald Harman Akenson. This helpfully provided a detailed look at the parochial economy, industry and culture of the parish, but on many occasions cited an earlier work by a gentleman called Dixon Donaldson. This was in fact first published as a series of articles for the *Whitehead News and Ballycarry and Islandmagee Reporter*, but was later compiled as *The History of Islandmagee* in 1927.

Upon obtaining a reprinted copy of this original work, suddenly the brick walls in my Islandmagee research began to fall apart. If we look to my Montgomery family in the parish (p.106), for example, Donaldson recorded a great deal on their history, noting that my schoolteacher ancestor John Montgomery was the son of a man who had moved to Islandmagee from the nearby town of Larne in the late 1700s to work on the farm of a Malcolm McNeill at Brown's Bay. Knowing the connection with this farmer has allowed me to further research his story.

Another useful resource for land research is the Periodical Source Index (PERSI) available on Findmypast (p.14), which allows you to search for the titles of some 2.5 million articles from historical, genealogical and ethnic publications around the world. In this instance, using PERSI, I was able to locate an article about the make-up of Islandmagee in 1817 by Samuel McSkibin, as published in an edition of the *Carrickfergus and District Historical Journal* (Vol. 5 1990). This included an incredibly detailed account of Malcolm McNeill's farm, but just about the only thing it did not do was to note the name of the manager that he hired to work the farm for him – i.e. John Montgomery's father.

The hunt continues!

# FURTHER READING

AKENSON, Donald Harman, *Between Two Revolutions: Islandmagee, County Antrim 1798–1920*. 1979, Gazelle Book Services Ltd

BLATCHFORD, Robert & Elizabeth (ed.), *The Irish Family and Local History Handbook*. 2012, Robert Blatchford Publishing Ltd

BLATCHFORD, Robert & Elizabeth (ed.), *The Irish Family and Local History Handbook 2*. 2013, Robert Blatchford Publishing Ltd

CLARKSON, L. A., *The Demography of Carrick-on-Suir, 1799*. 1987, Royal Irish Academy; Proceedings, Vol. 87, C, Number 2

CONNOLLY, S. J. (ed.), *Oxford Companion to Irish History*. 2011, Oxford University Press

DAY, Angelique, and McWILLIAMS, Patrick (ed.), *Ordnance Survey Memoirs of Ireland: Parishes of County Antrim III – 1833, 1835, 1839–40 Larne and Island Magee*. 1991, The Institute of Irish Studies and Queen's University Belfast

DONALDSON, Dixon, *History of Islandmagee*. 1927; republished 2002 by Islandmagee Community Development Association

DOOLEY, Terence, *The Big Houses and Landed Estates of Ireland*. 2007, Four Courts Press; Maynooth Research Guides for Irish Local History

GIBSON, Jeremy, and MEDLYCOTT, Mervyn, *Local Census Listings 1522–1930: Holdings in the British Isles (3rd edition)*. 2001, Federation of Family History Societies

GRENHAM, John, *Tracing Your Irish Ancestors (5th edition)*. 2019, Gill Books

GURRIN, Brian, *People, Place and Power: The Grand Jury System in Ireland*. 2021, Trinity College Dublin. (Accessible via https://beyond2022.ie/the-grand-jury-system-in-ireland).

GURRIN, Brian, *Pre-Census Sources for Irish Demography*. 2002, Four Courts Press; Maynooth Research Guides for Irish Local History

McGEE, Frances, *The Archives of the Valuation Office of Ireland 1830–1865*. 2018, Four Courts Press; Maynooth Research Guides for Irish Local History

MAXWELL, Ian, *Tracing Your Northern Irish Ancestors*. 2010, Pen and Sword Family History

MEEHAN, Helen, and DUFFY, Godfrey, *Tracing Your Donegal Ancestors (2nd edition)*. 2008, Flyleaf Press

MITCHELL, Brian, *A New Genealogical Atlas of Ireland (2nd edition)*. 2002, Genealogical Publishing Co., Inc.

O'NEILL, Robert K., *Irish Libraries, Archives, Museums and Genealogical Centres (3rd edition)* 2013, Ulster Historical Foundation

PATON, Chris, *British and Irish Newspapers*. 2013, Unlock the Past

PATON, Chris, *Tracing Your Irish Family History on the Internet (2nd edition)*. 2019, Pen and Sword Family History

PATON, Chris, *Tracing Your Scottish Ancestry Through Church and State Records*. 2019, Pen and Sword Family History

PRUNT, Jacinta, *Maps and Map-Making in Local History*. 2004, Four Courts Press; Maynooth Research Guides for Irish Local History

ROULSTON, William J., *Researching Presbyterian Ancestors in Ireland*. 2020, Ulster Historical Foundation

ROULSTON, William J., *Researching Scots-Irish Ancestors: The Essential Genealogical Guide to Early Modern Ulster, 1600–1800 (2nd edition)*. 2018, Ulster Historical Foundation

RYAN, James G. (ed.), *Irish Church Records*. 2001, Flyleaf Press

RYAN, James G., and SMITH, James, *Tracing Your Dublin Ancestors (4th edition)*. 2017, Flyleaf Press

SCOTT, Brendan, and DOOHER, John (ed.), *Plantation: Aspects of seventeenth-century Ulster Society*. Ulster Historical Foundation & Ulster Local History Trust

Various, *County Donegal & the Plantation of Ulster*. 2010, Ulster-Scots Community Network

**County guides**

The North of Ireland Family History Society produces a series of county research guides for the province of Ulster, available from **www.nifhs. org/product-category/booklets-county**.

Flyleaf Press also produced a series of guides for counties with the Republic of Ireland at **www.flyleaf.ie**.

**Familia**

The Ulster Historical Foundation sells copies of the various *Ordnance Survey Memoirs of Ireland*, from **www.booksireland.org.uk**, and past editions of its journal *Familia*. The following articles from Familia were of assistance in this book:

- AGNEW, Jean, *How to use the Registry of Deeds in Ireland*. Vol. 2 No. 6 1990
- ARMSTRONG, Deirdre, *The value of Ulster street directories*. No. 24, 2008

- COLLINS, Brenda, *Sources for a Seventeenth-Century Ulster estate: The Hastings (Irish) Papers in the Huntington Library, California.* No. 24, 2008
- MONTGOMERY, Ian, *The manorial courts of the Earls of Antrim.* No. 16, 2000
- SCARTH, Stephen, *Valuing the past: PRONI's online Valuation records.* No. 29, 2013
- SCOTT, Brendan, ROULSTON, William, and ROBINSON, Philip, *The Charter Towns of Ulster.* No. 29, 2013
- STEWART, Rev. David D.D., *The Scots in Ulster: Their Denization and Naturalisation, 1605 to 1634.* No. 11, 1995

# INDEX